When Christian Singles Mingle:

You're Just One Hint Away from Attracting the Love of Your Life

Edward J. Beck, Ph.D.

First published by Dog Ear Publishing
4010 W. 86th Street, Ste H
Indianapolis, IN 46268
www.dogearpublishing.net

ISBN: 978-1-4575-0848-6

This book is printed on acid-free paper.

Printed in the United States of America

TABLE OF CONTENTS

CHAPTER 4   GENDER ROLES IN CHRISTIAN SINGLES GROUPS

CHAPTER 5   THE HINTS

CHAPTER 6   INTRODUCING MR. BRAVE

CHAPTER 7   TO THINE OWN RATING BE TRUE

CHAPTER 8   ONLINE MATCHING SERVICES

CHAPTER 9   MISS-BEHAVIOR

CHAPTER 10   PROFILING CHRISTIAN SINGLES
                GROUPS

CHAPTER 11   THE "R" WORD

CHAPTER 12   IT'S ONLY NATURAL

CHAPTER 13   THE BIG BAD WOLF WANTS IN

CHAPTER 14   STEP INSIDE THE MAN-HUDDLE

CHAPTER 15   STEP INSIDE THE WOMAN-CIRCLE

CHAPTER 16   DON'T OPEN THAT CAN-O-WORMS!

CHAPTER 17   IT TAKES A VILLAGE...

Open Forum Discussion

Readers are invited to join in on the discussion on FaceBook. The group title is, "When Christian Singles Mingle". Alternatively, the author can be emailed at
ChristianSinglesBook@yahoo.com.
Your comments and feedback may inspire a second edition. To order books or make a payment for a book you already received go to PayPal.com and enter account number
DrEdBeck2000@yahoo.com
Books are $15.00 each and shipping is free.

Introduction

You approach the front door of the advertised meeting room. From a distance you can see a man and a woman standing there with fliers in hand ready to welcome anyone who ventures through the doors. With each step closer to the doors your heart beats harder as it drops down into your gut. Then it hits you like a ton of bricks: *Never in my wildest dreams would I have seen this coming—this . . . this . . . Plan B for my life.*

You sigh, then take a deep breath and remind yourself that the Lord brought you through a long journey to be here. So you choose to embark willingly on this Christian singles group, your new reality.

Christian singles (both never married and divorced) in the new millennium are finding themselves to be an ever increasing demographic in their community and church. When I first arrived at my first Christian singles group it was clear to me it was a community and had a heartbeat of its own. Attendees enjoy social aspects of church-sponsored singles gatherings, which are typically not attended by church elders, married couples, or teenagers. Consequently the common bond of singleness draws new people into the group.

The increasing divorce rate since the 1970s can explain much of this increase in the singles population. In addition, young college-educated professionals are putting off marriage till their mid- to late-twenties or later. It took me thirteen years to see a third contributing factor unrelated to divorce or delayed marriage—a common behavioral theme among three very large and distinct Christian singles communities. Despite the preponderance of attendees in the singles groups, few date each other and few leave the group to get married (to people they actually meet there). Hence, Christian singles groups appear to contribute to the increase in church singles populations by stifling...SOMETHING.

While the focus of this book is on the dynamics between men and women in Christian singles groups, the lessons apply to all single Christians. It doesn't matter if you attend a Christian singles group or not; if you are Christian and single you will benefit from reading this book.

What can possibly explain the low rate of marriages in singles groups? Hopeful married elders and pastors wipe the sweat off their brows exclaiming, "Phew!" with a wishful sigh of relief, when a new singles group is formed. They conclude that by allocating money and resources to put a bunch of singles together in a room, the Holy Spirit will pull back Cupid's bow and BAH-ZING marriage chemistry. This blessing might provide for some singles in their church but not so for the majority. The increasing singles population in Christian churches is a trend that the pastorate simply prays will resolve itself. Alternatively pastors seem unaware that facilitating the marriage process could sustain the long-term population and financial sustainability of their church.

Given the pastoral tendency to "turn a blind eye," singles are left to their own wiles to find a mate. Consequently, the unmarried flock grazes to the Internet in hopes of greener pastures. This grazing is despite the dismal odds of successfully finding Mr./Miss Right online. These two recurring patterns among pastors (avoidance) and singles (grazing) are not the main cause for the reduced rate of marriages coming out of singles groups. Then what's the problem? It's something missing from the behavior pattern of singles—a *spark* to catalyze an attraction reaction.

This book explains some behavioral patterns festering between Mister and Miss Right participating in Christian singles groups. I will point out causes that keep singles separated despite standing shoulder to shoulder at the same social gatherings and community activities. Along the way I will make broad sweeping generalizations and stereotypes of single men and women. The purpose in doing so is not to convince you that those observations apply to you. If a particular stereotype does not apply to you then thank the Lord and read on. If it does apply then take note and thank the Lord that you're not the only one to whom it applies; you're not alone. If you're not sure then ask a trusted brother or sister in Christ. The purpose of making generalizations and using stereotypes is to make a point. Simply acknowledge the take-home message and read on.

But don't fool yourself; you are reading this book for a reason. You can resist my perspective and laugh off the insights I offer or you can resist only to later "go down kicking and screaming," finally accepting what is presented. Given the controversial nature of my opinions, I fully expect a good percentage of my readership to go down kicking and screaming—but I'll accept even that kind of reluctant assent.

Feel free to question and discuss this material with the opposite sex. Do thirteen years of homework like I did. After you've done that, you may be ready to agree with me. If after much discussion you still don't agree with me, then write a book about your own insights and solve the elusive Christian singles conundrum yourself. You will not find this book in the financial shelves of your favorite bookstore. You will find it in the Religious or Self-Help sections. Thus, you also won't find any statistical analyses to corroborate my observations. No doubt you'll have to test my hypothesis firsthand before you implement my recommendations full-time.

This book is intended as a discussion piece between men and women. If I can get men and women talking to each other about singles' issues, then I will have partially succeeded in my purpose. To that end I have included provocative discussion questions at the end of select sections. The content and questions are unashamedly intended to stir up discussion and even controversy. Get together with a group of four men facing four women on comfortable sofas and read this book out loud one section at a time. If you don't like my discussion questions make up your own and have a blessed evening together. This kind of gathering works best over a potluck dinner. Indeed, if you don't like a man's opinion, you might just like his tuna casserole.

Many people have given me feedback on early manuscript versions of this book. Women say, "You sound bitter."

To that I say, "Amen, sister!"

Feedback from men includes words like moreover, furthermore, in addition as if to agree and extend the discussion to topics hot on their own mind. Hence, you can expect that other men feel the same way I do, or that they are frustrated with their church singles community in general or with women specifically. As such I have intentionally left the manuscript tone close to what is was when I first wrote it. I am a living, breathing, feeling Christian man and my attitude is a partial consequence of my Christian singles experience. As such, for me to hide an alleged bitter tone would be dishonest. Moreover, removing it would be selling out to a potential readership for the purpose of making money. Sorry . . . not gonna do it.

Finally, in his book on Christian singles ministries Dennis Frank offers his wisdom gained after thirty years in that area of service (Frank, Dennis. *Reaching Single Adults: An Essential Guide for Ministry.* (Grand Rapids, MI: Baker Publishing Group, 2007) 139). His recommended structure for ministering to singles, however, is not what I found relevant to my book. I don't intend to start such a ministry. What I found helpful were his side comments describing singles behavior and why he recommends a particular ministry technique. He writes:

"Single adults want to be told the truth about life and its hurts, complexities, and issues. There is no reason to beat around the bush with them. Issues such as sexuality, relationships, handling emotions, managing money, and other relevant topics need to be taught in a bold, frank, open, yet genuine way. They want to be told how it really is and will respect a teacher's honesty and candidness. Even when one may think the truth will offend them it is better to be honest and forthright."

But what is *your* part in your seemingly perpetual singleness? Andy Stanley in his Youtube video introduction to his book (*The Principle of the Path, How to Get From Where You Are to Where You Want to Be*, Nashville, TN Thomas Nelson, Inc. 2008) asserts,

"I've talked to countless people from just about every walk of life who have made terrible life-decisions under the assumption that their good intensions, their pure motives and their hard work would somehow trump the principle of the path and it never does."

The main thrust of Stanley's book is that the path you are currently on is the same path you will continue on unless you change direction in your life (hence the Principle of the path). Obviously, by direction Stanley means changing the *behaviors* in your life. You might wisely say that dropping subtle hints to attract the Christian love of your life is akin to "hard work". Maybe so but it is also consistent with God's creation of man (and down through lower branches of the phylogenetic tree). After all, man and woman don't come together in marriage and sexual union by random motion of body parts; decisions have to be made and acted upon with *behavior*. While praying will give discernment to future decisions and actions NOTH-ING will happen without your taking the first steps. So where is your current path of singleness leading you? Are you dropping hints in the direction of the path to marriage? Or are you praying without stepping?

I strive to be bold and frank in my honesty, even if that means offending you and consequently puts in jeopardy—if you are a woman—my chances of getting a date with you after reading this book. So be warned: If up to this point you have been mollycoddled in your Christian walk by your pastor, home-based weekly Bible study family, accountability partner, etc., this book will be an real eye-opener. Well, more like a "two-eyes-opener": one eye opened to its content and the other eye opened, perhaps a little blackened, by its delivery.

Upon embarking on this book, you will quickly notice the lack of scriptural references for support of much of what is written. Support for the author's statements comes from firsthand experience of human behavior, and as such your experience and opinions may differ. If you as a reader wish to pepper this book's contents with scriptural citations email them to me I'll include them in the next edition. No doubt my readers will have plenty to contribute to it.

About the Author

Dr. Eddie B. holds a Ph.D. in Cell Biology, with expertise in protein ion channel electrophysiology and interests in neuroscience. He has never taken a psychology or sociology course beyond introductory level. One exception is an advanced level undergraduate psychology course co-offered by the biology department titled "Brain and Behavior," the content of which is self-explanatory. He professes no other academic qualifications that might otherwise inspire the reader to sense credibility in what he writes. Nor has his scientific training been pivotal in formulating his arguments. However, his naturally keen sense of observation of human social behavior has been critical in developing the thesis of this book. Most significantly, since 1993 he has attended three independent singles groups sponsored by three major Christian churches in the mid-Atlantic region. The emerging theme that he observed in each of these three groups inspired him to write this book.

The author challenges you to consider his point of view. If you're a woman, he invites you to experiment with his suggestions and observe for yourself how men's behavior toward you changes. You might find that the author finally gives you the insightful pep talk for which you've been praying. If you're a man, this book will prepare you for your roll in stepping up to the dating "plate". Moreover, men will enjoy reading this book as if they, personally, are describing their own observations to the single Christian women in their church group.

Outside of Christian singles groups, Eddie B. enjoys swing dancing, park-and-pitch-style camping, river swimming, cliff diving, original song composition, singing in choir/worship bands, competitive volleyball, and creative writing.

About You, The Reader

The target audience for this book is single Christian men and women. However, many of my observations and comments are directed toward women. For that reason it is vital for men to read the entirety of this book so they can be up to speed with the issues and ready to chime in during face to face discussions.   Through conversations with many Christian singles I've noticed a few repeating themes. Could any of the following summaries describe you?

1. Deep down inside, you have an intense longing to meet the person of your dreams, Mr./Miss Right.
2. While you wait for him/her, you guard your heart, keeping it safe from being harmed.
3. You refrain from overtly pursuing Mr. Possibly Right (i.e. making a beeline for him whenever you see him, asking him out on dates, effusively gushing over him in after-service conversations, etc.) because you desire the affirmation of being pursued.
4. While waiting for Mr./Miss Right, you put up the facade that you are not preoccupied with meeting him/her to avoid looking too desperate, too needy, or too available. Simply stated, you want to avoid appearing as if you are living a life that is not Christ-centered or not having faith that God will provide.
5. You believe that the Lord will intervene in the life of Mr. Right, to put you and him on a common path, an unmistakable collision course for each other.

6. You know Mr./Miss Right when you meet him/her, because in a matter of moments visions pass through your mind, such as worshiping the Lord together, marriage, family, college graduation, empty nest, and retiring to the front porch swing with grandchildren in your lap.

7. You view church attendance as consecrated strictly for the purpose of praising God and for becoming edified by God's Word. Any desire or behavior (even if only subtle) that might lead you to focus on the opposite sex is contrary to keeping church attendance consecrated for God—unless, of course, it's THEE ONE.

8. Any man who takes action to meet you at church violates your sense of consecrating your church attendance, and therefore, he cannot be Mr. Right unless, of course, he is dashing in every way you've dreamed he would be.

9. In the appropriate circumstances you still don't show Mr. Right any genuine interest, because if he is a man of God he will pursue you undaunted by your lack of expressed interest (vocally, through body language, etc.).

10. You have a friend or relative who is single.

If you said, "Yes, that's me," to even just one of the above summaries, then this book will be a page-turner for you.

MALE (M) OR FEMALE (F) QUESTIONS:
- Are you presently attending a Christian singles group?

- What earthly "rewards" did you hope God was going to bless you with as a consequence of becoming a Christian? Marriage? Family? Fame? Fortune?
- What is your current state of expectation or fulfillment of your hoped rewards?

CHAPTER 1

LIFE CYCLE OF A SINGLES GROUP

CRITICAL MASS THEORY

It wasn't long into my experience with Christian singles groups before I formulated my critical mass theory. It describes the progression from inception to final demise (i.e. critical mass) of a Christian singles group. I present my theory at this early point of the book for a reason: establishing credibility. In the "ABOUT THE AUTHOR" section, I make an effort to convince you of my observational powers. That effort is for the purpose of establishing credibility with you. You rightly should be asking me, "Why should I give any credence to what you have to say?"

The following description will hopefully have you concluding, "Gee! I never thought about it that way, but the dynamics of my singles group does indeed reflect his description of critical mass. Maybe he has other observations from which I could benefit." If you are not currently in a Christian singles group you will benefit from reading this chapter so that you are in-the-know; if you ever do attend such a group you will be prepared. You'll be able to quickly recognize and evaluate the status of the group and gauge whether or not your time spent there will be fruitful.

Typical of an organized scientist, my critical mass theory is broken down into phases, much like pharmaceutical companies do for their drug approval process. For you, embracing this theory might indeed be a bitter pill to swallow (pun intended).

PHASE 1: CORE GROUP (linear rate)

In the beginning of a Christian singles group a small handful of energetic, young, single, attractive, and socially gifted people—the core group—decide to get their friends together for Christian fellowship. The core group tells their friends, who by some unwritten law of human nature (birds of a feather flock together?) will also be energetic, young, single, attractive, and socially gifted.

PHASE 2: RAPID GROWTH (exponential rate)

Within a few months of weekly meetings the group experiences rapid growth in attendance numbers. Word of mouth spreads fast when a "hot-spot" for meeting singles is found. Christian men and women are no different from the secular when it comes to a desire to find someone for love and marriage. That is, they will go where they might find a suitable mate. The main difference is that Christians will naturally desire a mate who is also a Christian. Rapid growth of the group will generate a feeling, as if a new pulse of hope is revived in the love lives of its members.

As good as rapid growth and a new pulse sounds, a word of caution is in order. Your vivacious group may be at risk of being labeled by the skeptics. Indeed, some idealistic Christians may refer to such venues as "meat markets"; as a clever retort I refer to them as "meet markets." Clearly, Christians must meet before any essence of community can develop in their group. Thus, idealistic Christians who call a singles venue for Christians a "meat market" are not seeing the greater potential of the group. Instead, either their own motive for attending is suspect or they are simply jealous— possibly after experiencing rejection—that others can feel so free about meeting other Christians. If this "meat market" attitude is true for you, then you probably don't belong in a Christian singles group; you're probably just putting a damper on the vibrant group dynamics. (see Chapter 10, WHO BELONGS IN A CHRISTIAN SINGLES GROUP?)

In addition to rapid growth, "mate choice overload" also characterizes Phase 2. Mate choice overload is simply defined as indecision due to too many competing choices. My description smacks of a person in the "market" for a new cell phone, for example, overwhelmed with the available choices. Likewise, in the group, a man/woman sees a number of men/women that he/she would like to date but ends up home alone on a Saturday night due to indecision. I call such indecisive men benched batters (in the dating analogy to baseball a man, the batter, must step up to home plate to bat, which is the equivalent of stepping up to a woman to ask her out). He is home alone or benched because 1. He's overwhelmed and can't decide on which woman to ask out; and 2. By asking one woman out, he might lose the perceived interest of the other women should it not work out with the first woman. Women can also be described as benched batters but for entirely different reasons. Indeed, those reasons are the focus of this book and will be discussed in subsequent chapters.

Despite the lack of dating initiative in the group, during the rapid-growth phase there is still an intense feeling of relationship possibility. The feeling is like nothing felt before for Christians who are hopeful of finding a spouse. Phase 2 could also be called the addictive phase because for many the euphoric feeling of relationship possibility (with both new friends and Mr./Miss Right) is far more exciting than the reality of settling down and committing to just one person.

PHASE 3: PAIRING-UP (saturation)

During Phase 3, the most attractive and socially adept singles will begin to pair up. After a year or two of feeling the intense excitement of relationship possibilities in Phase 2, they decide, "Okay, my options are not going to get any better than this." Ideally the men make a mate selection, and the couples begin to leave the group to develop relationships with hopes of marriage. Thus, their presence can no longer contribute to the intense excitement and vitality of Phase 2.

PHASE 4: PRECIPITOUS RATINGS DROP (decay rate)

What characterizes Phase 4 is attraction factor attrition. Let me explain. Let's call the attractive and charismatic people who start the group in Phase 1 "tens" on a one to ten rating scale of beauty, charisma, etc., with ten being the most attractive. In Phase 3 it is the tens who ideally pair up and leave the group. It's not long before the original tens in leadership of the group are replaced by the "next generation" of leaders. The likelihood is that charismatic tens don't last very long in this group because ideally they attract the "ten" mate they desire and leave the group to develop a relationship with hopes of marriage. The next generation leaders take up the vacated leadership positions yet they probably won't have the same level of attraction as the originals. Thus, "nines" will begin to populate the leadership team, ushering in attraction factor attrition.

Over the course of a few years, say between five and ten, successively less and less attractive/charismatic "generations" replace the leadership team. And because the people they invite into the group are their equals, the attraction factor of the entire group also drops. Meanwhile the tens, nines, eights, and sevens have long since either paired up and left the group, or they simply left because there were no more of their equals from whom to choose. A greater likelihood is that the female tens, nines, eights, and sevens leave the group because (for various reasons addressed in this book) there is little dating activity going on and they go in search of more aggressive men. And when the women leave, the men follow. Phase 4 ends with the commencement of a swift decline in the attraction factor and a near simultaneous reduction in the number of people attending the group.

> TIME OUT: How are you doing so far with my critical mass theory? Are you at all surprised or concerned how I, a Christian, can look at other brothers and sisters in Christ and proclaim or judge them to be a "ten" or a "seven" or a "four" on the beauty scale? (I have more to say about rating yourself on a scale of beauty in

Chapter 7, Dr. Eddie B's Laws of Minimizing Rejection). Have you concluded that I, your brother in Christ, am seemingly unable to love other Christians without regard for their outward appearance?

Honestly, I am also concerned that I can be so governed by "physical chemistry" instead of by a spiritual connection for another person. I wrestle with knowing the part that superficial attraction plays in God's plan for uniting, in life-long compatibility, a man with a woman.

Despite my wrestling, while I agree that loving people unconditionally is what Jesus calls us to do, Christians are still earth-bound, hormone-filled sacks of conflicted joy. We have both the joy of the Lord—spiritual—and joy of the physical. If at this point in your life you believe that other Christians will gravitate toward you only because of your inner beauty, then this book will likely be your icon of innocence lost or simply a good reality check.

My innocence was lost in a different way, the day I realized that most single Christians put forth a good church face (i.e., say, act, and perform accepted Christian standards); we don the template of Jesus to attract a mate (i.e., I am spiritual). But when it comes to choosing Mr./Miss Right, a completely different set of standards kick in.

The search for Mr./Miss Right is guided by one standard. Realizing our *physical* soul mate takes precedence over realizing our *spiritual* soul mate. It's a natural desire, and therefore a gift from God. Disagree with me all you want, but all your objections won't change human nature, especially *male* human nature. So if/when a man explains to you that the hand of God Himself ordained his interest in you (part of his church face), it would be fair to say to him, "You're full of phony-baloney. I think you're just physically attracted to me." Similarly, when a woman rejects a man because he's not "the one" God has set aside for her (her church

5

face), we men can tell her, "You're full of phony-baloney. I think you're just not physically attracted to me."

Wow! This TIME OUT really cut to some core speculation of human motivation. Do you need to pause and reassess, or do you pretty much agree with my take on the role of physical chemistry in your relationships, past, present, and future?

My second motive for discussing Critical Mass Theory at this early stage (first reason is to establish credibility in my power of observation) is to establish my writing tone. To that goal, I broached the topic of physical attraction and Christians. I chose this topic because in my experience it is *"thee"* topic of conversation that Christians like to evade the most in an effort to put on the best church face. This topic is analogous to parents of a young teenager evading the topic of sex.

In this book I'm communicating at my best when I write what I feel from deep within my very male physical body and mind. If you have never experienced a man—father, brother, lover, friend, etc.—brave enough to do that with you, then this book is your chance at a fresh realistic look at men. TIME IN.

PHASE 5: CRITICAL MASS (group demise)

By the tenth year, the profile of the leadership and the members of the Christian singles group suffer a ratings drop in the fives or lower. I call this group of people the "socially awkward," because invariably they are fives or less on the attraction scale, extremely socially challenged, and very needy. Moreover, attendance is at a point where the elders of the church begin to question the outreach value of the resources budgeted for the group. Simply stated, critical mass is realized when the remaining members look around the room at each other and say to themselves, "There isn't a single person in this group to whom I am attracted. I'm outta here!" And true to my definition of socially awkward, as they leave the room for the last time the walls become unstable because there is no one left to hold them up.

That last sentence is a play on the phrase "a wallflower holding the walls up," which describes a quiet, introverted, socially awkward person. At parties they are described as simply holding up the walls because their backs are usually pushed up against them and out of the way of people actually having fun, mingling, and/or dancing.

After a meeting to determine the fate of the group and much prayer, chairs and tables in the meeting room are folded up and rolled into storage. It's the end of the group—critical mass.

M/F: In which phase do you see your Christian singles group? Why? Is attendance expanding, leveled off, or declining toward critical mass?

M/F: Upon becoming a Christian, were you sure that other Christians would no longer be drawn to you or reject you according to your physical appearance?

AGEISM IS A COFACTOR

Besides ratings drops another factor that determines the speed at which a group heads to critical mass is member age. Many Christian singles groups have an advertised age range. Others just have an implied age range based on the name of the group—for example, "Twenty-something" or "Thirtysomething" or "College Quest" or "Barren Life Together"— or the teaching topics or the age of the pastor or the themes of the social activities, and the like. A Christian singles group without an explicitly advertised age range will tend to draw out singles both older and (though rarely) younger who won't fit into the average age dynamic of the group.

Let me comment on the older singles. Just as in any population of people, some of the older singles will defy their age by keeping fit, being energetic, socially graceful, and physically desirable—to name a few characteristics. Such singles generally fit in well with the Christian singles group and attract others of similar desirability to the group. They increase the duration of Phase 2: RAPID GROWTH. The majority of the older singles, however, (especially in the USA) tend to have the opposite effect; they decrease the duration of Phase 2 leading the group much more quickly to Phase 5: CRITICAL MASS.

I remember attending a Christian singles group advertised for folks in their thirties and forties. It seemed to me that most people were in their forties and fifties or older. One guy was so old that he was sitting near the snack table in his own world with slobber running down his chin after having chowed down on the food. I think he was actually asleep. After attending this group three or four times, I concluded that it would not attract the woman that I was hoping to meet. I stopped going. The group reached critical mass shortly thereafter. For that reason it is wise for Christian singles groups to not only advertise an age range but also to have strict enforcement of the age range. If doing so means having two Christian singles group in your church, then so be it. Occasional mixer social events can always be arranged to include both groups for increased opportunity for finding mutual chemistry.

Case in point: I attended a Christian singles group for about ten years and, therefore, I knew there were people who aged-out of the group but would not leave to join the next older singles group. One day we got a new pastor for our group that was early into Phase 4: PRECIPITOUS RATINGS DROP. Recognizing that many in the group had aged-out he decided to establish an upper age limit on the Christian singles group *and* enforce it. Many were disgruntled to have to step up to the next older singles group in the church. The pastor made an unpopular decision, but it was the right decision. Sadly, however, many of those who were sent to the older singles group were in leadership positions. Moreover, the number of members in the targeted age range had dwindled over the years, probably due to the presence of too many aged-out members. Thus, the poorly timed age restriction may have led the group to Phase 5: CRITICAL MASS. I am no longer in touch with that group, so I don't know its fate.

In summary, without age limit enforcement from the beginning, the average age of the group will only increase by more than one year every year. This trend is due to natural human aging of its members and inclusion/acceptance of more and more older new people in the group. In addition, once the group's average age becomes skewed toward the upper age limit the people in the lower age limit will begin to leave the group. They'll leave due to a preponderance of age-out members who simply should not be there. Moreover, prospective new attendees in the lower age range will not come out. Hence, without attendees in the lower age limit the average age becomes skewed beyond the upper age limit.

The take-home message here is that without a stated and enforced age range for a singles group at its inception, the average age of the group will only go up. Moreover, when you let long-time members stay after they have "aged-out," it's an invitation to others who are over the age limit to join. When the majority of attendees in a singles group is no longer in the specified age range, younger singles will not attend, and critical mass is inevitable.

How then is ageism a cofactor? It is an acute cofactor. I can't think of any other aspect of the Christian community that is as acutely age-cognizant as the singles groups are. Yet when members of the singles groups volunteer for child care positions, soup kitchen rotations, clothing drive collections, hospital visits, etc., they are not so much motivated with the hope of meeting Mr./Miss Right. In fact, in my experience I have always been a bit relieved walking into a volunteer church activity that was populated with a cross section of the church members from kids to seniors. It just felt more like a place where reality and the Gospel was going to play out. I was much less concerned about being on the watch for Miss Right.

Nevertheless, when I'm at my singles group, the presence of even one aged-out member will irk me to no end. It's hard to explain, but it has something to do with Phase 3: PAIRING-UP where the group is enjoying the relationship possibility addiction. The presence of aged-out members simply "bums that trip." Women become negatively preoccupied with being asked out by someone their father's age or close to it. Maybe some women stop attending for that reason. Also, when I see anyone or any activity that will negatively impact the age-cohesion of the group, I'll get very irked. Simply stated, I get that way because I am 100 percent convinced that the Lord will provide the woman of my desires from this group. I don't want any "threats" to the group that might make her run away or decline to attend in the first place. In short, what's at stake is my marriage possibilities and, therefore, my future God-glorifying sex life in marriage. That's why I get irked.

One sister in Christ corrected me on the age issue. She said something to the effect that women should not be concerned about who might ask her out at the singles group. If the men who are asking her out are older than the age she prefers then she should simply say no graciously and keep praying for her Mr. Right. But leaving the group just to avoid having to say no graciously is classic immaturity. I fully agreed. I have much more to say about such immaturity in CHAPTER 11: JUST SAY IT and the other sections surrounding it.

M/F: Has the average age of your singles group reached the advertised maximum upper age limit? If it has what do you believe will be the impact on prospective new attendees who would enter at the lowest advertised age range of the group?

CHAPTER 2

FORWARD THIS MESSAGE TO YOUR SINGLE PASTOR AND CHURCH ELDERS

Let Me Be Painfully Clear

Your singles pastor and church elders are most likely married. Hence they may need to hear it again. It would be most effective for you to broach the topics of this chapter with them. Alternatively, encourage them to read this chapter; it's only 4 pages long. By including this section I do not admit to having previously written in an ambiguous style. Simply stated, the take-home message of my critical mass theory *must* take root in their very married brain. Here it is.

First, upon starting a singles group it is imperative to advertise the targeted age with a specific age range, for example twenty to thirty-four. "Twenty-ish to thirty-ish" and the like will *not* suffice.

Second, a system must simultaneously be instituted for verifying that each person attempting to set foot in the group is indeed in the targeted age range (i.e.. enforcement).

Third, it must be a matter of known policy that when a member reaches his/her thirty-fifth birthday (for a group advertising 34 years maximum age) he/she must exit the group meetings, no exceptions, no ifs ands or buts, no grace periods or grandfather clauses. If these three criteria (explicit age-range, enforcement, and exit strategy) are incorporated into the weekly singles group bulletin then members have enough forewarning to prepare for their swan-song exit out of the group.

12

M/F: Do you believe it is contrary to Christian doctrine to ask an aged-out member of the group to "retire" from the group?

WHAT'S IN A NAME?

It's important to notice what is *not* vital advertisement criterion. The group's goals, mission statement, biblical precedents, select Scripture verse, or purpose are all perfectly okay to state. Indeed, such Christ-centered statements would surely be viewed as a suitable "representation" by the sponsoring church. However, if your pastor holds the conviction that singles will be attracted to the group first by its mission statement, he is foolish and has surely forgotten his life as a former single person. Most singles I have talked to dread being single and can't wait to be married. Therefore, it would be unproductive for the church to deem marriage motivation as an incompatible reason for joining the group. The name of a group is a mere drop of water compared to the sea of marriage motivation on the minds of attendees and those yet to arrive.

In fact, as far as future church attendance, tithing, and sustainability is concerned, the church has every motivation to help its singles find spouses. They desire to marry, settle down (probably nearby), raise a family, and attend church, maybe even become leaders there. I write more on this topic in Chapter 17, WHAT CAN CHURCH LEADERSHIP DO TO HELP? and others places. Suffice it to say that if a Christian church is the singles group sponsor, certain beliefs and behaviors are surely implied and expected. Thus, a mission statement while appealing and/or trendy is unnecessary.

YOUR CHILDHOOD BEDROOM IS NOW AN OFFICE

If your pastor disagrees with even one of the three criteria (explicit age-range, enforcement, and exit strategy), tell him that he should be prepared to start the group all over again in five to ten years. Think of it this way. What is the effect of the following statement from parents to their sixteen-year-old child? "When you turn eighteen, you can live with us free of charge whether or not you go to college, whether or not you have a job, whether or not you have any aspirations for your future." With such an attitude, how are the parents motivating their child to adult independence? What if from age sixteen the parents instead remind their child that, "After high school graduation you can only live with us if you are enrolled full-time in college. Otherwise you have to move out and get a full-time job. We can help you get started with this check for . . ." Such statements give the child fair warning and plenty of time and motivation to make preparations for graduation day.

Similarly, fair warning of an exit strategy for leaving the Christian singles group will motivate the attendees to prepare for the day that they age-out of the group's advertised age range. Prior to that day, near aged-out members will hopefully be more proactive about stepping up to the dating plate instead of basking in the addiction of relationship possibility and fellowship described in Chapter 1, Phase 2: RAPID GROWTH.

WHEN PC FAILS

Warning: I have written and erased the remaining sentences in this section several times but cannot find the right "politically correct" words. So here it is, unapologetically.

Dear Singles group Pastor,

Because you are on staff with your church, you are implicitly expected to be and are, perhaps, over-indoctrinated with the concept of showing compassion for other's needs even before being concerned about your own needs. This selflessness is indeed biblical. However, when selflessness is applied in a mollycoddling manner that creates unhealthy dependencies, it is no longer biblical. Because it is mentally easier to mollycoddle than it is to use discernment, pandering to people in need may dominate one approach, when in God's eyes a little tough love or accountability would be demonstrating true Christian compassion. For example, do you have the conviction to take an obese or nicotine-addicted member of your church aside and say the following? "Tom, your lack of attention to your physical body, God's temple, is leading you to disease not to mention lack of self-control."

If *you* don't have that kind of conviction to ask new singles group attendees for age identification then *you* are leading the group to the disease called critical mass. I repeat: If *you* don't have the conviction to ask new singles group attendees for age identification then *you* are leading the group to the disease called critical mass. Consider age identification as disease prevention for your singles group in which you want to demonstrate compassion for people in the advertised age range. Now *that's* putting the group's needs before your own. If after reading my arguments you see my point but still don't have the gut-level conviction to ask for age identification, then delegate that job out. Ask someone in the lower age end of the group to do it; she will be more than happy to help preserve the group's age cohesion.

CHAPTER 3

SECULAR BEHAVIOR DIFFUSES INTO CHRISTIAN SINGLES GROUPS

SWITCHING GEARS

Enough of my observations on phases and points of organization and beauty ratings and telling singles pastors how to do their difficult jobs. The following sections will focus my observations on human dynamics of Christian singles groups, not their attendance numbers or ages.

But first, in order to understand human dynamics it's important to understand the culture in which the dynamics are playing out. In the United States the politically correct "police" have made it clear that tolerance of other's political/religious beliefs is crucial for harmony within our culturally and intellectually advanced society. I agree. But such tolerance implies that while at my nine-to-five job I don't go around trying to aggressively convert everyone to Christianity. Thankfully, such tolerance also implies that Muslims, Buddhists, They-ists, Them-ists, and Satanists will also refrain from going around aggressively trying to convert people at work. This result to me is a desirable benefit.

The long and short of it is that we as Americans have learned a sixth sense that subconsciously instructs us when and where to be evangelistic and/or charismatic in our love for the Lord. But zeal for the Lord is definitely welcome and encouraged at our churches and Christian singles groups.

Unfortunately we don't have as strong a sixth sense for checking our American culture at the door of our Christian gatherings. Outside influences will inevitably be reflected in the dynamics of these bodies of Christians. As you read ask yourself, "Is the described behavioral dynamic in my singles group a consequence of our secular culture or a consequence of the principles of God found in the Bible?"

KEEP YOUR EYES ON THE PRIZE?

Let's say you have recently become a Christian. God has blessed you. And now you have found your way to your first Christian singles community. Prior to attending the singles functions did the following scenario regarding your love life after becoming a Christian play out in your imagination? It did for me.

Imagine you're the winning contestant on a TV game show. Now you get to choose a prize from behind one of three big doors. God is the game show host with wireless mic in hand.

> GOD: And now, Sally, your reward for accepting my prodding to become a Christian is waiting for you behind each of these three doors. You get to choose which godly man will enter into marriage with you till death do you part.

> *(The audience claps and cheers in anticipation of seeing the three men.)*
> GOD: Let me describe these three godly men to you, Sally. Behind door number one is Tommy B. Goode.

> *(The door swings open revealing a stunningly handsome man in his mid twenties. The women in the audience gasp as their hearts throb. Sally cups her hands over her quivering mouth.)*

17

GOD: Tommy holds a degree in electrical engineering with a minor in biblical counseling. He volunteers in his church's children's ministry and heads up a volleyball outreach Sundays in the park.
Now, Sally, let's see who's behind door #2.

(The second door opens revealing the next man, Justin T. Yu. God proceeds to rattle off some pretty equally impressive credentials, as well as for the third man behind door number three named Parker N. Close. Sally is physically overwhelmed with the decision she has to make. Finally she looks at God.)

SALLY: God, I am too overwhelmed by your goodness reflected in these men. How can I possibly choose one over the other?
GOD: Yes, Sally you just said the blessed words. Of course I knew it but now the audience knows, too, that you are a truly humble person. So, Sally, you don't have to choose; I'll do that for you. After all who else knows you better than I do?

(God turns to the audience and loudly and excitedly yells out.)

GOD: Who's your daddy?!

(The audience shouts out in unison.)

AUDIENCE: *You* are . . . *You* are . . . yay!

(God capitalizes on the opportunity to whip the audience into frenzy. He immediately raises his arms victoriously in the air hopping up and down as if a boxer after winning a fight and runs all around the studio virgin white clothes flowing in his wake, high-fiving audience members and motioning them to start a wave from one side of the auditorium to the other. It's pandemonium. Then everyone is standing and jumping up and

down in their place in unison with God's tempo. He's bringing down the house! It's a foretaste of worshiping God in heaven here on earth. He finally makes his way back over to Sally who is shaking with anticipation over knowing who she will spend the rest of her life with.)

GOD: Sally you don't have to make a decision; I'll do that for you. Actually I've known about this moment since the beginning of time. I've been looking forward to this day for . . . ever! I know you and everyone in this studio better than you know yourself, so isn't it fitting that I should select your man for you?

SALLY: Yes, God, yes! Let's do this!

GOD: Okay, give me a moment to put it on your heart to *know* which is your man.

(In a moment Sally and Justin T. Yu shout each other's names at the top of their lungs as they run for each other ecstatic with open arms. They finally collide into each other as they wrap themselves tightly in each other's arms. Sally's feet fly into the air as Justin spins her about. The audience is again in pandemonium.)

GOD: Whoa! I knew there would be some heavy chemistry between these two. Ho Ho HO HOOO! Get a rooooooommmmmmmm and a marriage minister, but not in that order.

(God rushes up to them.)

GOD: Now let's not get carried away. I mean, after all I know you two, but you two just met each other. Arm's length apart now. I gotta' be able to slip my written word, the Bible, in between your bodies.

So what's the point of that childish fantasy?

When I became a Christian, I thought my reward was going to be a beautiful Christian woman who would soon become my wife. Forget about everlasting life praising God, I just wanted a beautiful wife. After all, I'm committing my life to the Lord, a life filled with obligatory bonding with overly sensitive, domesticated, tamed married men, boring outreach events, square dances, and a bunch of rules. Isn't God going to reward me with a beautiful woman to endure the Christian life with me?

No kidding. That's what I was thinking.

Does any of that sound familiar to you at all, I mean the game show skit? Are you waiting for your spouse "reward"? Do you hold a certain image in your mind and heart about the heaven-sent person you will marry? Would you have become Christian as willingly if you knew ahead of time that God had set aside for you only an average person with an average income, average looks, average sense of humor, average taste in clothing style but with above average delight in the Lord? Women who keep their eyes on the prize —Mr. Musing, who is found only in their imagination —neglect to inspire the real men around them. Furthermore, uninspired men leave women asking a resounding question about men. That question is asked below.

M/F: What was your expectation before joining your singles group that the Lord would show you your future spouse? What about after a year or more of attendance?

THE MILLION-DOLLAR QUESTION

What do the following things have in common? Rotary telephone, vinyl records and turntables, black and white TV, "till death do we part," and feminine vulnerability. Yes, that's right; today they are all more or less reflections of past US culture/lifestyle, nothing more than nostalgia, antiquated notions, or Smithsonian museum relics. But the greater question of interest is as follows.

"Eddie B., what's wrong with the men in this group? Why aren't they asking anyone out?"

Sherri, a trusted gal-pal of mine from my early years of Christian singles group attendance, actually asked me this question. I was at first surprised at her candor because the "right" Christian attitude in the group was one of non-expectation of meeting Mr./Miss Right. "I'm waiting faithfully on the Lord to provide" is likely an unspoken mantra in many Christian singles groups. My response to her at that time was genuine, but I have learned so much more about the answer to her question since then. I was a new Christian at that time by about a year or two. But before I answer Sherri's question, let me describe a little about what *my* "mantra" was.

When I arrived at that Christian singles group I felt that the Lord, through the group, would surely bless me, in His time, with a wife. I was in my twenties with a master's degree and very desirous of finding Miss Right and settling down to marriage and whatever else the Lord would provide through it (meaning children). All my life, even through my rebellious late teens/early twenties, I looked ahead to the day when I would be done with being single and married with children.

Maybe that goal was kind of ingrained in my brain since I was from a large family. Nevertheless that was and still is my dream even now some years later.

Discussions with many singles since then have led me to believe that most Christians have the same marriage goals. Thus, my answer to Sherri's question might also represent *most* Christian men. So what was my answer? It's complicated but simple, and I answer the question in no uncertain terms throughout this book. As the following account suggests I'm not the only man that has heard this question from women like Sheri.

F: Do you feel that the men in your group are too docile with regard to their motivation to date women?

M: Are you reluctant to ask out a woman in your singles group? Why/why not?

From Brent, a Fairly New Christian

Brent started out his Christian walk in a Bible study. As you will read, he was pretty much feeling isolated from the main body of believers in his church. One day he went on a beach retreat for the church singles, and he was surprised at his observations of the women there. Here is Brent's short report.

"I became a Christian, of course, in December 2002, but really I didn't get 'plugged in' at church until at least this past summer when I got involved in softball and small group Olympics. So I went through a good eighteen months of being a Christian where the only Christians I could ever talk to were a few guys from my small group and a few friends. I had a few female Christian friends, but they were all taken. I always used to wonder why I never met any Christian women—I *saw* them at church all the time, I just didn't *meet* any of them. Because I didn't meet many Christian women, I dated secular women—but I felt if I talked about my own faith on dates or in the context of the relationship, they'd think I was getting preachy and get rid of me. (In fact, a couple of them did get rid of me when they found out I was 'religious.')

" 'Round about August, I started dating a secular girl I was quite excited about. There were some scheduling difficulties, and I discovered that the only weekend in September that she was *not* out of town was the weekend I was scheduled to go to the church beach retreat. I seriously considered skipping out to be able to spend time with her, but I decided that a commitment was a commitment and I had to go. Anyway, at that beach retreat I must have met a dozen lovely Christian women, and then in the subsequent couple of weeks I must have met a dozen more. And then sometimes you hear them complaining about being single, and it's just amazing, because these are attractive women—in the secular world there would be guys all over them.

"The contrast between these girls—sweet, nice, kind, etc.—and your typical secular woman couldn't have been clearer. Needless to say, quite quickly I lost interest in pretending not to talk about Christ with my secular date, and things there faded away. I'm still not dating a Christian girl, but I've certainly decided that I *should* be, so now it's just a matter of figuring out how to go about doing that."

Brent observed attractive Christian women lamenting the lack of man-initiative in their being asked out for dates. When I first read this report from Brent I thought, "Maybe those women wanted Brent to ask them out."

F: Do you feel that those lamenting women were probably interested in going out on a date with Brent? Why/why not?

ARE YOU SEEING STARS YET?

Not long into my experience with Christian singles group, I discovered that the men aren't very assertive at asking women out...for anything, let alone a date. Before writing this book I took a naive approach to solving this problem. One year at a costume party (Halloween to secular society) at the end of October I dressed up as Cupid. I was replete with wings, tights (actually heart spangled boxer shorts over red long johns), ivy wreath around my head, a bow and arrow. For the arrow I used a sawed-off broomstick with a boxing glove on the arrow end of it to literally "stick" men with it at the party saying, "See that girl over there?" (BONK!!!!!) "Now go fall in love with her." Who's going to argue with Cupid? I definitely made lots of men and women uncomfortable that night. On two different occasions I actually won an award for most creative costume. You can check it out on YouTube. Search my account EJB111 and Cupid.   Since even Cupid was unsuccessful at motivating men to ask out women I decided to examine the women in the group. Were they typically homely? No way! Were they inordinately consumed with following the letter of Christian "law"? I don't think so.

HEAR ME ROAR

Upon reflecting on the influence of secular behavior in Christian singles groups where is that influence coming from? It's coming from mass media! How do you think an intelligent being from outer space would view women given the following media-portrayed adult woman's attitude as portrayed by a variety of advertisement media? Imagine these words being spoken by a woman who wants to be, or more precisely expects to be, asked out by a man in a Christian singles group.

"I am woman; hear me roar" (Reddy, Helen and Ray Burton. "I am Woman". *I am Woman*. Capitol Records, 1970).

"You've come a long way, baby." (Virginia Slims™ cigarettes introduced in 1968 by Philip Morris International with ads allegedly targeting girls/women).

"I can bring home the bacon and fry it up in a pan." (Lyrics changed and based on the song by Leiber, Jerry and Mike Stoller. "I'm a Woman". 1960. For Enjoli perfume ad. for Revlon introduced in 1978). I kid you not. Check out this YouTube video: **http://www.youtube.com** search jA4DR4vEgrs

"Because I'm worth it." (L'Oreal company slogan)

What about how men from earth view women? Here's my biased composite of women's attitudes that I have sensed in TV shows and commercials, movies, read about or simply experienced first-hand. "It's my prerogative to change my mind. My gender has gone through great pain to earn rights equal to those of men; you better treat me like royalty and the best thing far above sliced bread. I am so focused on enjoying my newfound rights and enjoying the pursuit of my independence/career that you ought to be thankful if I coincidentally cross your path, even if I don't notice that you are there. *You* want to ask *me* out? Excuse me? Do I even know you exist? You must first fully devote your attention to me, conquering my beloved obstacle course that I have set up between us like my career, dreams, life expectations, standard of living, independence, girlfriends, fairy tales, and romance novels, not to mention the social standing and economic power of my father. In fact once you get beyond these obstacles, I will rebuff you whether I'm interested in you or not, just to keep you on your toes and to remind you that I'm a modern-day woman. Besides, I'm supposed to play hard-to-get in order to make you appreciate and respect me, right?" Are you this woman or know someone like her?

Yeah, you might be saying that the word *right* at the end of that paragraph pretty much negates all the sentiments that precede it. That "right?" indicates a life-long indoctrination by mass media in conflict with the Proverbs 31 woman. While this Scripture is directed at the "ideal wife" it has equal application to single women. Moreover the academic accomplishments, career ambitions, financial independence...etc of single women are consistent with a Proverbs 31 woman. What's absent from a Proverbs 31 woman are the attitudes reflected in my biased composite written above for modern day women.

M/F: What does the impact of mass media have on your Christian attitude? The things you buy? The job you have? Your general life-style?

M/F: Which causes you greater anxiety: 1) publicly breaking a code of Christian conduct or 2) publicly wearing a striped top with plaid skirt/pants to your singles group or office party? Why? What concept do you feel this second question is getting at?

ALL THAT GLITTERS IS NOT GOLD

In case you haven't figured it out yet, we men are beginning to roll with laughter. We are laughing at women who think that having equal rights in the work world (among other places) is having some kind of grand privilege. Well, we welcome you with open arms to take over swinging this sledgehammer against the cement eight hours a day, mopping floors, laying bricks, driving bulldozers, programming computers, managing people, painting bridges, designing skyscraper, selling pharmaceutical drugs, representing the voice of the people in politics and on and on. Ninety-five percent of men in this country would gladly give his job to his wife because most jobs just don't provide that much satisfaction. Besides we wouldn't mind adding a few years to our life expectancy by eliminating work-related stress.

The only reason most men go out and do their less than inspired nine-to-five job is because it makes them feel like they are "out there" doing something useful for their wife and children. By my estimate only about 5 percent of all Americans have jobs that are so satisfying that they would do it for free if they didn't have bills to pay. Outside of this 5 percent are men who love not their job but love what their job affords them (house, boat, hobbies, family, etc.). *You* are also probably not part of this truly gratified 5 percent. So tell me, how do you like your job? Do you see yourself doing it till you're sixty-five then reflecting on it the rest of your retired life with utter satisfaction?

Given the high standard of living in this country it's likely that if you marry and start a family you will be too used to your standard of living to quit your job. How many guys are there in your Christian singles group that will be able to afford a stay-at-home wife and kids? Will he be able to afford you a standard of living to match the one you have now? If you own your own home or rent your own apartment, you might be spared some of the "pain" of a single income family when you marry. I mean, you and your husband will still have to write out that monthly housing check. But based on your penny-pinching lifestyle before getting married (i.e. you had to pay your own hefty housing check) you will know how to adapt to his income. This scenario applies just as well to stay at home dads.

But don't fret; I have good news. If you are blessed with a happy marriage, going to work to your oh, so gratifying job (tongue in cheek) won't seem so purposeless. It supports the well-oiled and meticulously maintained machine of your marriage, that is, if you *are* married. If you are not married, I speculate that you are heading for the grand disillusionment of the past forty years of improved equal rights for women. You will be experiencing what men call "midlife crisis." Not only will you be single, alone, and bitter, but you will also be stuck in an ungratifying job that has long been necessary for maintaining your "liberated" lifestyle.

Does that sound bleak? I think so, but it's the reality for many, many American men both single and married. No, I have no solution, but I can say that leading a Christian life devoid of greed, vanity, destructive pride, and excessive pampering can ease this bleak outlook. But the whole point of all this career lecturing is to point out that you don't have to go through it alone. If you want to go through it with a companion husband, you had better check your attitude and start learning that Mr. Right is not part of the Equal Rights Amendment package. You have to accommodate him not impress, compete with or ignore him.

Throughout this book I use the terms pride, productive pride and destructive pride. When used alone, pride simply defines a potential emotion or state of mind. Productive pride is an emotion realized in statements such as "I'm proud to be an American," or "I'm so proud of you, son," or "the pride of home ownership." Apostle Paul feels pride in his work. "In Christ Jesus, then, I have reason to be proud of my work for God." (Romans 15:17, *The Holy Bible*. English Standard Version). He also instructs, "Do all things without grumbling or questioning, that you may be blameless and innocent, children of God without blemish in the midst of a crooked and twisted generation, among whom you shine as lights in the world, holding fast to the word of life, so that in the day of Christ I may be proud that I did not run in vain or labor in vain. (Philippians 2: 14-16, *The Holy Bible*. English Standard Version)

Destructive pride on the other hand is an emotion realized in statements such as "No one gets away with making me look foolish in public," or "No one can tell me what to do," or "It's my way or the highway," or "I don't need your help." C. S. Lewis simply uses pride in place of destructive pride:

"Unchastity, anger, greed, drunkenness, and all that, are mere fleabites in comparison: it was through Pride that the devil became the devil: Pride leads to every other vice: it is the complete anti-God state of mind." (MERE CHRISTIANITY by C.S. Lewis copyright © C.S. Lewis Pte. Ltd. 1942, 1943, 1944, 1952) 122.

"He (Jesus) said that some (prideful people) would preach about Him (Jesus) and cast out devils in His (Jesus) name, only to be told at the end of the world that He (Jesus) had never known them. And any of us may at any moment be in this deep-trap" Ibid:124

When I use the term pride it is with the understanding that in the beholder it is neutral until he/she takes it to either productive or destructive emotions or expressions. Suffice it to say that when I call someone full of destructive pride (as Lewis would agree) he/she is an offense to God, a sinful emotional state.

F: Have you ever related to the following expression? Hell hath no furry like a woman scorned. What were the circumstances?

M/F: Can you remember a time when another person evoked your destructive pride even if only known to you? What did you think, say, do or feel about it?

CHAPTER 4

GENDER ROLES IN
CHRISTIAN SINGLES GROUPS

THE HYPOTHESIS

If it's true that women have "copped" an attitude of fierce independence and self-importance with their equal rights how can they temper (but not get rid of) that attitude so as to be more accommodating to men? That brings us back to Sherri's question:

"Eddie B. why aren't the men asking anyone out?"

My answer is in the form of the following hypothesis.

Women today have lost the fine art of dropping godly, subtle hints tailored to specific men that interest them.

Are you shocked and amazed by this simple hypothesis? Maybe you're disappointed. But don't dismiss this assertion just yet.

While I offer a list of such godly, subtle hints in another chapter (see Chapter 5: HUMAN EQUIVALENT OF PHEROMONES: THE HINTS), it only includes those that I can place my finger on. I'll leave it to women to figure out other hints because honestly that's the woman's department not a man's. Women either have to be wise enough to learn from other women or you can learn by trial and error. Either way, *just do something*!

Shortly after starting into this paragraph I recalled a feeling that I sensed and a subsequent conclusion that I once made. I was only one year into my attendance of my first Christian singles group as a new Christian. After realizing that not much dating or many courtships were happening in that group, I remember looking around and thinking, "Man! This is a sterile and barren group of Christians." Yet the group attracted many eligible singles to it. It was mind-boggling at the time. But now I know that what was missing was nothing more than women's godly, subtle hints delivered to men that interest them. This hint dropping sentiment can be phrased in a hundred ways but I think you get the essence. In the end it all comes down to dropping hints.

This lost art of hint dropping seems to coincide with the appearance of women who would scold a man either verbally or silently for his "old fashioned" attitudes (for example, holding doors open for them). That's an example of how our American culture has diffused into the room of Christian singles group meetings. Do you regard hint dropping as an antiquated notion of your grandparent's generation? If you burn with sexual desire as Paul advises it is incumbent upon you to take godly steps to satisfy those desires.

"But if they cannot exercise self-control, they should marry. For it is better to marry than to burn with passion." (1 Corinthians 7:9, *The Holy Bible.* English Standard Version)

Your hint kick-starts the whole process.

What other biblically acceptable way is there to start the attraction process? For the purposes of this book there are no other ways. I have more to say about this hypothesis throughout the book. Indeed, advising women to drop hints is the cornerstone of this book. Can you believe that the solution to a sterile singles group is that simple? I suspect, however, that convincing women to start dropping hints is not as simple as flipping a "hint" switch. Hence, much of this book will be stories, anecdotes and opinions. Hopefully they will convince you to fully consider my hint-dropping hypothesis.

F:	How does the following hypothesis strike you? Women today have lost the fine art of dropping godly, subtle hints tailored to specific men that interest them.
F:	Does that hypothesis seem undignified?
F:	Do you feel it is your role to drop hints?
F:	What do you feel is your role in attracting the attention of Mr. Right?
M:	Can you tell when a woman is dropping a hint to you? What goes on in your mind when you detect a subtle hint on your radar?

THE BASEBALL ANALOGY

I would be remiss if I didn't include a sports analogy to illustrate the rationale behind my hypothesis. I know; seems odd for a book with an audience predominantly consisting of women. Nevertheless...

Among men it is commonly said that when a man musters the guts to ask a girl out, he is "stepping up to the batter's plate". In this analogy the plate is home plate as in the game of baseball. About 95 percent of the game is focused on two people, the pitcher and the batter. The pitcher throws the ball from a mound of dirt sixty feet away from home plate. The batter stands beside the plate with a bat determined to hit the ball thrown by the pitcher. That's all you need to know for this baseball analogy.

A man steps up to the plate to ask out a woman. You may have even heard a shorter version of this analogy among your single female friends. "The guys in this group ought to start 'stepping up' and ask us girls out on dates."

Indeed, as a man I see this problem as a man's problem. We men *absolutely* need to start stepping it up. But let me tell you. In baseball a batter would probably not step up to the plate unless there was a pitcher on the mound with a ball in hand.

In my analogy the pitcher is actually a woman. And from my point of view there are no women making their way out to the pitcher's mound. Well actually, there are many women on the mound, but they forgot an essential piece of equipment—*the ball* (a woman's hint). As such it's pointless for a man to step up to the batter's plate. If women are not throwing pitches very few men will be stepping up to the dating plate. Yet there will be some men stepping up to the dating plate even if they don't receive a pitch and you will soon read why those men are probably Mr. Wrong (see Chapter 6: COLD-TURKEY and HE'S MR. BRAVE BUT CAN HE LEARN?).

F: Have you heard this baseball analogy before? Are there other analogies that women would more likely understand that also make this point? If so discuss them.

SOMEONE ELSE ALSO SAID IT, SO IT MUST BE TRUE

The Eldredge couple writes a special section to single women on the topic of dropping subtle hints (Eldredge, John, and Stacey Eldredge. *Captivating, Unveiling the Mystery of a Woman's Soul,* Nashville TN, Thomas Nelson, Inc. 2005) 163-164. They write the following.

"As one young woman wrote to us, "I am afraid that I and numerous other women have interpreted womanly purity as 'completely ignore the man you are interested in until he proposes to you.' "

And why, then, *would* he propose to you?

Of course a woman should be alluring to the man she is attracted to. A smile, tenderness, an interest in him and his life are natural and welcome. To look your best; awaken him to your presence. Yes, you can offer beauty to him—in gently increasing amounts as he pursues and comes closer. And yes, there are parts of you that should be held as mysteries until he fully commits, and you offer yourself to him on your wedding night. Don't offer everything, but don't offer nothing.

How much, and when? That is more than we can say in a chapter. Walk with God. Be a wise and discerning woman. Be aware of the issues that could cause you to hold back or give too much. Invite, arouse and maintain your personal integrity."

WOMEN'S EARLY EXPERIENCE WITH HINT DROPPING

Why would any woman disagree with their role as godly, subtle hint droppers? Women similarly experiment, not with outright pursuing boys but with simply dropping hints early on in childhood. Bouts with getting no response or attracting Master Wrong, however, changed her perspective. Women will thus minimize the behavior (i.e., dropping hints) that led to the unpleasant experience (being ignored by Mr. Right or being pursued by Mr. Wrong). This reaction to heartbreak is the same reaction boys and men have to rejection. You now avoid that behavior of hint dropping as an adult because you learned as a child that it gets you into heartache trouble.

I could just as fairly say to men, well then, suck it up; that's life. Go ask women out cold-turkey! It's *your* role as a man. But that makes women uncomfortable (when it's from Mr. Wrong) but subtle hints from women by definition do not make men uncomfortable. Besides, your subtle hint is what kick-starts the dating process; a man's leadership role lasts the rest of the relationship. Hence, women should see the role of dropping hints as a very small but vital part of the much bigger marriage picture.

I WILL DROP HINTS BUT MR. MUSING ISN'T HERE YET

When I discuss hint dropping with women they insist that they *do* drop hints when their Mr. Musing is present. Mr. Musing (described in more detail in Chapter 15, A WOMAN'S FANTASY) doesn't exist, yet, he is who a woman imagines marrying one day. Are you convinced that you don't have any reservations about dropping hints to Mr. Musing? If not that's wonderful but don't stop reading this book just yet.

Would you agree that you're waiting for at least one Mr. Musing to arrive before you start hint dropping in your singles group? If so you had better beware. First, by waiting for Mr. Musing you contribute to the atmosphere of sterility in the group. Second, you develop a reputation of being so picky that you are clearly waiting for the second coming of Christ so you can date Him. Unfortunately for you He is already married to the church.

I know; you don't have to tell me. I am fully aware that the previous paragraph oozes with unthinkable sentiments such as "lowering your standards" or "settling for Mr. Less-than-Musing." I don't like the way it sounds either. However, would you say that you're at a point in your Christian conviction where you understand the essence of "taking up your cross to follow the Lord"? Can you fathom that your cross might just be to marry Mr. Less-than-Musing, who happens to be of good Christian character? If you're like me you would rather remain single the rest of your life than marry someone whom you consider to be your "cross."

I have to confess that I don't know anything about the likeness of the mental image Christian women have about their Mr. Musing. As I just said many men would guess that women's man-template is Jesus; others would guess that it's Mr. Hollywood. Perhaps it's a combination of the two templates. Whoever a woman's man-template is in her mind he's not with her now or they would be engaged or married. So here's what women can do to not only help themselves take their eyes off the prize (Mr. Musing) but also add a little fertilizer to their Christian singles group. Start dropping hints to Mr. Maybe; not Mr. Repulsive, but Mr. Maybe. Let's say five out of ten of those men pick up on the hint and invite her out for conversation and fellowship.

She helped herself in that now she has five men showing some initiative and making her feel desired. She is still hoping for Mr. Musing, but she plays her hint-dropping role to these Mr. Maybes nonetheless. She goes out on a few dates and learns a little more about men *and* herself. Indeed, the leadership that her date demonstrates, even if she doesn't feel chemistry, just might be the human interaction that catalyzes a change of heart. Miraculously, a woman might find after five or six different dates that her template of Mr. Musing changes, even if subtly. She helped herself and simultaneously helps the group because she demonstrates to other women that if they drop some hints they, too, can have dates. While he may not be Mr. Musing he could be Mr. Right.

F: What proof can you offer that you don't determine Mr. Musing solely on the basis of secular values such as looks, income, ability to win friends and influence people, college degree, etc..? To prove it recall who you dated, talked to, befriended, etc., in high school, college, work, singles group.

F: Which men do you spend—or hope to spend—more time talking with at your social events? How do you decide on them?

TAKING MATTERS INTO YOUR OWN HANDS

In summary, don't do it!! I am adamant that women should *never* ask a man out for a date even if it's just coffee. For one, even a good Christian man may have a challenge not taking advantage of your expressed interest in him. Second, I have personally experienced that when a woman asks me out I relinquish my leadership responsibilities to her. I'm not suggesting that I started wearing perfume or that I expected her to start opening car doors for me. It's more a mental thing. For reasons that I don't understand, my mind goes into this mode that seems to say, "Okay I didn't ask her to be here with me, so she better make this night entertaining and enjoyable."

Let's assume for the sake of argument that a woman-initiated date eventually turns into marriage. Do you want to be married to a man who looks for excuses to eschew his leadership responsibilities? A woman asking a man out for a date just might desensitize his sense of leadership judgment for years to come. Maybe it won't. Do you want to take that risk?

The few experiences that I have had with women asking me out taught me something really important. When men take women out on dates we work hard to be nice, entertaining, interesting, exciting, somewhat romantic, polite, etc. Indeed it is hard leadership work, but it is a joy when a woman exposes her vulnerability by dropping a hint to him to get the ball rolling in the first place.

To men's frustration it seems that women have the timing of dropping hints a bit mixed up. The time to drop hints is when you want to have a date. After you are married then you communicate your heart's desires verbally because you have the relationship security to do so. (i.e., no fear of rejection). Yet how often do your hear men complain, "My wife got upset that after her many requests to take out the trash I still didn't do it. I insisted that she never once asked me. Then she said, "By now you should know what that certain look on my face means!"

So take advantage of the power of dropping hints while you're still single because after you are married your husband will rightly expect more direct means of communication.

BUT I WANT TO BE PURSUED

That's a fair desire for a woman to have. It's written in enough books that men like the challenge of the pursuit whereas women like the feeling of being pursued. I can be very easily convinced that it's in the design of our gender and therefore God's plan for us to be that way. But when women drop hints do they violate this apparent natural order of things? No.

By analogy in lower animals the female gives off olfactory cues called chemical pheromones (i.e. a hint to the males). From my neuroscience classes I learned that some lower animals have more developed brain regions than humans that confer to them a very keen sense of smell. That's why they use certain dogs to pick up the trail of an escaped convict and to sniff out people trapped in collapsed building rubble. Instead of an overly developed olfactory brain region, humans developed a forebrain, which is the brain region that functions in sensory integration, complex planning, and abstract thinking among others. As such humans are conferred, in addition to instincts, the mental capacity to think and reason. So use your mind and think of some creative ways of dropping hints. Such mental capacity for doing so is unique to humans, and remember: a mind is a terrible thing to waste.

The combination of your creative thinking and my enumerated suggestions for hints should get his "pursuit" ball rolling for you. Let me make it clear that dropping hints is not akin to pursuit. Do not call him on the phone, making a beeline to him the moment he steps into the room, nudging his car with yours, or asking him out on a date. These are not female hints but pursuit behavior reserved for men, except for the nudging of cars, and that wouldn't come from a man because we are simply too practical. Nevertheless, there is plenty of manly follow-up pursuit behavior for a man to indulge in once he feels the slightest bit "invited" by you. Your hint will clearly pale in comparison to his overt pursuit behavior. You won't have to doubt that dropping a hint to your future husband was a blessing to your marriage. You won't be tempted to think, "Gee, if only I hadn't dropped that subtle hint to get him to notice me, maybe he wouldn't be so [fill in the blank] as my husband." With your subtle hint you are simply opening up your door just enough to let a guy step his foot in.

Yet some women may be rebuffing guys even after they open the door the slightest crack (in the form of a hint); we guys will pay our pursuit dues in the form of prying your door fully open. These dynamics are akin to salsa dance lessons: one step forward, one step back. You give a hint, the guy steps forward in pursuit; you give a rebuff the guy steps back to regroup. You give another hint, the guy steps forward in pursuit; you give a rebuff the guy steps back to regroup. While learning the dance the guy will be wearing down your defenses, his confidence being fueled by nothing other than your hints of interest. In short order he will stop stepping back despite your rebuffs. However, rebuffing behavior can be a tricky tactic as described Chapter 13, THE RULES.

A pursuing man will be building confidence in his manly pursuit behavior, and you will have your womanly needs met by feeling pursued. For some men your initial hint will be enough to ignite his pursuit behavior to a kindling passion; subsequent rebuffs on your part will not faze him. Other men, on the other hand, may need additional acorns presented to him. A squirrel that is scared off once by your rebuffing behavior may be very reluctant to approach you again. An intuitive seventh sense on the part of women is useful at helping you decide the timing and the degree of the hint/rebuff dance that you orchestrate. As a man I can't (and shouldn't) guide you any further on that dance floor. Moreover, I'm not wholly convinced that you should rebuff a guy that you are interested in.

Rebuffing behavior by a woman can be OK after a relationship is well under way. She explicitly explains to the man that she wants to feel pursued by him and that her rebuffing behavior is simply playful tests for him to pass. But without her explanation such rebuffing behavior can end a relationship.

YOU CAN'T HANDLE IT ANYWAY

My final angle on the benefits of hint dropping vs. expecting a man to ask you out cold-turkey is as follows: You simply can't handle being asked out by anyone except Mr. Musing, not even Mr. Right.

I make this statement based on experience. Women generally don't know how to reject a man in a dignifying manner. Most women simply lie or evade giving an answer altogether. You just can't handle dealing with rejecting a man. Ironically, your body language doesn't lie. I have witnessed a spectrum of body language ranging from delighted to horrified by my date invitation. There's actually not much in between those two extremes. Just like a light switch a woman is either on or off (delighted or horrified respectively).

It's *way* beyond the scope of this book to instruct women on how to change their subliminal body language simple because I don't know how to teach that. But just as a picture paints a thousand words so a video paints many fold more words (each "frame" of a video is one picture and there are roughly ten frames per second). As my dad would recommend, find a guy who will help you practice by asking you out while being recorded. You can review the video and observe your body language making desired changes for the next take.

Just to prove that women can't handle rejecting men in a dignified manner pick up a pen and paper and describe the way you generally reject men who ask you out cold-turkey (that is, the men who are not Mr. Musing).

What did you actually say to him? Take a few minutes; I won't go away. (Cue *Jeopardy* countdown timer sound bite).

Time's up. Did you write something down? If you read your sentences to Jesus would He be glorified by your treatment of men? My own answer to this question was not esteeming. As a rule I would typically accept one date with a woman who asked me out. But if after the date there still wasn't any chemistry I wouldn't accept another date.

Suffice it to say I know it's not easy to reject someone. If women could reject men in a manner that is dignified and actually instills a little awe in the man—awe of the woman's character—then I don't have a problem with a woman's cold-turkey expectations from men. But I highly, very highly doubt that women can be taught or even trusted to respond in this manner. Therefore, I strongly promote the hint-dropping alternative. You just can't handle dishing out rejection in a manner esteeming to men.

OLDER WOMEN WITH YOUNGER MEN

I have not done a statistical analysis on the apparent trend of older women marrying younger men. My gut instinct, however, prompts me to hypothesize that there is indeed an increase in the number of married couples who fit this description. Moreover, terms such as "cougar" corroborate this notion at least in the secular singles world. Nevertheless, in a society where men typically have the attitude that "the younger the woman the better," it's curious that this apparent older woman/younger man trend exists. What societal factors could have changed men's minds toward pursuing older women?

Two factors come to mind immediately: 1) the increasing divorce rate; 2) women waiting till later in life to marry. These two factors alone have increased the number of single older women in this country. But that doesn't explain how older women are able to attract and marry a younger man. I believe single women in their late twenties to mid thirties wake up one morning to a harsh reality. They're getting older, getting more set in their ways, buying pets, getting physically less desirable, and realizing the count-down ticking of her biological clock. To top it off they begin to realize the grand disillusionment of how their career accomplishments are indeed financially profitable but sadly not very gratifying.

So you get up out of bed on that harsh morning and look in the mirror to find that all you really have is wrinkles and dark streaks and some expensive products to cover them up. You will realize that you've been blessed with many things, but you are still lacking the most important thing (after a relationship with God) and that is marriage and family. For women who put equal importance on their relationships with other women, I say you are headed for more heartache than you think. Yet I don't deny the incredible value that same-sex friendships add to life. It's just that same-sex friendships are not the final end that the Lord intended for us. Same-sex friendships are valuable in their own right and even more valuable in preparation for a marriage relationship with the opposite sex. So after you turn away from the mirror on that harsh morning, it hits you like an epiphany and you resolve, "This year I'm going to find me a man to marry."

Such epiphanies, reality checks, wake-up calls (call them what you will), and subsequent resolutions are a gift from the Lord. What else could possibly convince you to switch gears while moving full steam ahead in the direction of uncertain reward in your career as a single person? So here's what you do. You start to observe and appreciate the incredibly rich resource you have for meeting Mr. Right. And that resource is quite simply your womanhood. It is your generally higher-pitched voice and softer vocal delivery. It is the way you let your hair down to play as a lively backdrop to the soft skin of your neck and shoulders. It is the way your eye contact with a man when prolonged by just another second causes him to melt like soft music tames a lion. It is the way your body language changes when you're around a man for whom you feel a certain physical attraction. And the more you tear down the sterile pillars supporting your gender-neutral professionalism (that are so important to have as a career woman) the more you realize how beautiful and effective your feminine mannerisms are at attracting Mr. Right.

I view women as having three choices. You can remain single and full of destructive pride or you can humble yourself and find the man of your dreams. By humbling yourself I strictly mean that you are now ecstatic to drop hints. You don't even care if those twenty-something-year-old women call you undignified behind your back. Can you see them all huddled over there across the room of your Christian singles group while men are falling over each other to be near you? Ironically, you may have been one of those huddled women ten years ago. In essence you have been blessed with the conviction that God has given you certain attributes to attract a man and attract a man you will. This attitude is obedience to God's design, not defiance. Amen.

Women's third choice is to remain single and full of pride in knowing that your life is dedicated to being single while glorifying God by serving the poor and the unreached in foreign countries. I am admitting here that being married is certainly not the end-all for men and women who are called to the mission field (either as singles or as married couples). Don't misunderstand me though. Both married couples and singles can serve the Lord equally right where they are. My point is that if you are single, not actively dropping hints to men and not actively plugged in to serve, I mean REALLY serve the Lord you will end up neither married nor serving the Lord as a single person. You are in life-limbo, waiting for life to happen to you instead of taking active steps in faith towards either marriage or service unto the Lord. Of course married couples are not exempt from service to the Lord; it's just that there are more variables for married couples to resolve, children and in-laws, for example.

As one of those other women huddled in the corner of the room ten years ago, you might have read books like this one. But now ten years later you tell yourself, "Gee, that author was right about that hint dropping thing. Men are very easy to attract with that approach." So while the younger women are bolstering up their destructive pride in the corner of a Christian singles group, you are ten years older and enjoying the attention of the younger men that would naturally gravitate to those women in the corner had those women dropped some hints of interest.

Along with dropping hints to younger men, older women also give up on the fantasy that a prince in shining armor (Mr. Musing) will ride up to her on a horse to sweep her off her feet. Moreover, that ever-growing criteria list of features she wants in Mr. Musing gets tossed to the wayside in favor of a REAL man (Mr. Right) replete with faults, weaknesses, and trivial unattractive attributes. My guess is that our criteria list only gets longer and longer as we get older and older, not because we are "getting to know what we like" in the opposite sex but because we don't have the opposite sex in our lives. Surely getting to know the opposite sex in a friendship or dating relationship will show all of us how silly some of our criteria are once we experience the warmth of companionship.

F: Do you find yourself drawn to men that are five or more years younger than you are? Do you see them as a chance to recapture lost time? Do older men or men your age seem to be too set in their ways for your criteria list?

M: Have you ever experienced the allure of an older woman who knows how to drop hints? Does her behavior make it a joy to ask her out for coffee or does it make you want to run away from her?

MEN AND SQUIRRELS

In another episode of *Seinfeld*, *"The Rye"* (*"The Rye"* Seinfeld. By Seinfeld, Jerry and Larry David. NBC. 1996) an interesting take on men's fear of rejection is presented. In essence men are like squirrels. They won't walk up to you, and they tend to run away if you approach them. In that episode, Elaine, a single woman, comments about how men are like timid squirrels. "I'm trying to get a little squirrel to come over to me here. I don't wanna' make any big, sudden movements. I'll frighten him away."

Let me take it a bit further. You've got to be holding an acorn if you're even going to stop him in his runaway tracks. To men the acorn represents whatever it is that he finds irresistibly attractive in a woman. Now just imagine if by your gentle and nonthreatening manner you coax a squirrel to come within about a foot of the acorn in your outstretched hand. Now imagine that after ten more minutes, the squirrel is six inches away and you suddenly without warning jump up and scream out, "Boooooooh!!!!!" The squirrel darts away even before your feet touch back down to the ground.

Women who don't drop hints to the guy they are interested in meeting are doing the equivalent of saying "Booo" to a squirrel otherwise eager to approach her. Yes, you do indeed have the acorn, but you are unwittingly also giving us the big "Booo." Indeed that's the kind of survival instinct we men have for avoiding rejection.

You may not know that you are saying "Boo". After all, you're just sitting in a chair doing nothing more than just breathing and staying awake. How can this posture be saying "Boo"? Just believe me. If you're not dropping a hint, you're clearly saying "Boo" to men. The sooner you accept this reality and start dropping hints, the sooner you'll have men happily eating the acorn, your hint, from your outstretched hand.

Men's Innocence Lost

What defining moment in the life of males sensitizes them causing them to run away like squirrels from females? In my male shallowness, I want to equate a man becoming sensitized (or losing his innocence) with a woman losing her virginity. But just what male innocence am I talking about? I'm referring to the innocence of a naive little boy. Do you see him as he approaches a female kindergarten classmate or the girl next door for the first time in his life? Depending on the outcome of his pursuit of her, he will be scarred, indifferent, or encouraged. Since most kindergarten marriage proposals won't last very long, he will probably be indifferent or scarred. Because of the great fear of rejection that most adult males have, I will continue with the assumption that something scarring occurs.

By the end of the week, his fantasy of living with her in his cardboard box fort in his playroom is dashed and his innocence is lost. Life growing up in America is for most kids pretty sweet; that is, we don't suffer a lot of tragedy and emotional pain before the age of fourteen or so. As such, we boys experiencing the loss of our innocence at a young age can be a poignantly defining moment to our future manly psyche. Perhaps the sting of a failed kindergarten marriage proposal is the only real reason for us boys to understand and believe the common phrase, "It's a cruel world out there." Indeed, despite all that our parents do to keep us safe from harm, we boys can lose our innocence with a simple naive kindergarten marriage proposal.

The last two sections about squirrels and kindergarten marriage proposals are an effort to give women some insight into the male psyche. Rejection does not bounce off our chest like bullets off of Superman. Despite our rational, logical exterior we men are also sensitive. Therefore it is important for women to step up to their role of dropping hints. An interested man will detect your hint and follow through with a date invitation since you gave him some indication that you will say yes.

F: Did you ever receive a kindergarten proposal? Do you remember the interactions between the two of you that lead up to the proposal? Do you remember how you felt about the boy before his proposal? Did your behavior toward him in any way lead him to believe that you would say yes? How did you feel after he proposed? How long did that feeling last?

M: Did you ever tender a kindergarten proposal? How did it go? How did you feel afterward? Did you do it again?

CHAPTER 5

THE HINTS

WHAT HINTS SHOULD I DROP SHORT OF A LEAD BALLOON?

If women want to get men's noses out of the feeding trough or out of a sports huddle they have to emit a pheromone that men can detect. Yes, perfume does help, but that won't do by itself. Emitting pheromones works for animals, but it's a rather weak strategy for humans. Perfume in combination with a hint is even better.

This brings up some logical questions. 1) What kind of hints am I talking about? Can I describe some for you? 2) Why shouldn't women hold out for Mr. Musing? After all, you're worth it, right?

HUMAN EQUIVALENT OF PHEROMONES: THE HINTS

Of all the topics that I have discussed over the years with single women, the most difficult request has been for me to describe godly, subtle, well-crafted hints. Indeed, a well-crafted hint is what gets the dating ball rolling between two people. "Wild West" TV shows and movies exemplify this concept the best. When a woman wanted to attract the attention of a man, she would drop her lacy handkerchief in his path. He would kindly pick it up for her and the conversation would start. Today, however, women might think that it would take dropping a lead balloon in a guy's path to get his attention. Another rich tradition of hint dropping was recently called to my attention. It's called the "language of the fan."

The fan is a handheld paper and bamboo stick-folding contraption that we Americans would attribute to the Japanese or Chinese culture. In the closed configuration, the fan resembles about fifteen Popsicle sticks stacked on top of each other. On one end a rivet, or equivalent, holds the sticks together that allows them to spin around the rivet. A half-moon piece of paper, typically with an attractive print on it, is pasted to the sticks that are interspaced equally to give support to the print. Returning the sticks back to the stacked condition folds closed the print, keeping it hidden from the eye, not unlike compressing an accordion to the fully compact condition.

I'm not about to do a literature search to figure out if the language of the fan is history or folklore. Nevertheless, I will describe it. It's quite simple. When fans were fashionable, women used them to deliver messages to someone across the room or across the saloon, whatever. The degree that it was fully opened or closed and positions in between meant something. The way she held it in her hand and over her face meant something too. Now imagine that the man she fancies looks in her direction and they make sure eye contact. She would quickly flash out a quick message just for him then look away from him as if her fan gesture was simply coincidental. Depending on the message, and his interest, he would pursue her or leave her alone. You can do a search online to learn more about the language of the fan and the top ten fan hints.

Unfortunately I don't have a top ten list of hints for you. Though I do have some ideas. And a guy like me shouldn't have a top ten list or those hints might be too overt. The point is that your hints are supposed to be subtle enough such that the guy doesn't realize you're giving them. Only guys that are already interested in you will detect them if only subconsciously. For argument's sake let's assume that I am exceptional in my ability to detect such hints, whether I'm attracted to the woman giving them or not. Here's what I've observed as good hints.

1. Make yourself available to conversation. If you are attending a Christian singles group, don't clump up into a group of women. I realize that there's safety in numbers but doing so makes you completely inaccessible to men. Besides, you're at your Christian singles group; how much safety do you need? If a guy isn't likely to approach you alone—fear of rejection—then it's only reasonable to conclude that he's not going to approach you with an audience watching him. Just remember that before and after a man approaches a woman he wants to meet, he already hears in his head everyone in the room, including you, laughing at him for the very thought that you would tell him your name, let alone accept a coffee date with him.

2. Men actually like to see women in groups but not all the time. So go ahead; clump up. But remember most guys will not approach you until you are at least a step away from earshot of other women. I'm not suggesting that you go sit in a dark corner of the room waiting. I'm saying that you've got to demonstrate that you can make friends with other women while also making yourself accessible to meeting new men by peeling yourself away from the clump periodically.

3. If your eyes make contact from across the room don't look away too quickly. Linger on his eyes a bit then release. But before a second goes by look back at him. Is he still looking at you? If so then flash a smile. If not, keep looking till he notices that you are still looking then flash a smile. Afterward, go quickly back to what you were doing before you saw him or your hint will no longer be well crafted and subtle.

4. When you engage in conversation, maintain eye contact that lasts longer than your average eye contact. But don't hold on so long—four-second rule—that he starts to think you might be trying to hypnotize him. Most women will know precisely how long is just long enough.

5. There's an age-old woman's beauty product on the market. It's not Estée Lauder, Avon, Maybelline, etc. In fact no one company has a trademark on it and it's free to you. Over generations and generations it's been a sure-fire facial enhancement that gets a man's attention immediately. It's called a smile. Do you remember how beautiful your smile was the first time that one older boy looked your way? You couldn't hold it back if you tried. So while you talk with Mr. Possibility, exercise your right to smile. If he attempts humor, smile a little more, even if what he says is not humorous to you. Your laugh might loosen him up and his confidence might spill over into better joke-telling timing and delivery. You know how important those elements are to a good joke. Finally, unlike shoes, jeans, hairstyles, or catch phrases, your smile never goes out of style. Wouldn't it be safe to say that if you're not smiling that something is wrong? When you first meet someone or in the first few moments of a conversation if a smile is not in there somewhere there is something wrong. I would conclude that such a woman is simply untrusting and bitter for the way things ended up the last time she flashed a smile at Mr. Wrong. Clearly bitterness is an anti-smile and a sure anti-hint. I recently heard a related interview on National Public Radio (NPR) circa March 2011. The interviewee was a woman photographer who specializes in portraits for professional purposes (Facebook, LinkedIn, business cards etc..). She claimed that photographing men was so much easier than women. For women it takes the right make up, the right lighting and angle

(to mask unwanted age indicators) and smile to capture the essence of whom she wants to portray. For men, age indicators are assets and a neutral facial expression is perfectly acceptable even demonstrating confidence. For women, however, lack of a smile means coldness. Period! I emphasize that I just paraphrased the woman being interviewed.

6.   Ask him questions about...him. Your personality will dictate the type and subject matter about which you will ask. Any expression of interest on your part is good. I once complained to my elder married sister that the single women I have talked to don't know how to carry on a conversation. I explained that I find myself asking lots of questions but not getting any in return. I am often tempted to say to a single woman at the end of our monologue, "Well, enough about you. What about me?" My sister suggested that instead I have a quarter handy in my pocket. After you ask a question and she is finished giving her answer hand the quarter to her and say, "Now you have the question quarter. It's your turn to ask me a question." So the quarter gets passed back and forth with both people contributing the to the question/answer session. Overt yes, but if I actually did try this with a woman she would be much more aware of her self-absorbed focus and hopefully ready to dialogue like an adult with the next guy who dares to try.

7.   Prevent random friends from cutting in on your conversation. This suggestion is crucial and in fact the impetus for getting this book started. One time after church service I was engaged in conversation with a single woman, Rachael, I had met the day before at a small group picnic. After the service we were at that moment of awkwardness in between our hellos and polite greeting and the more interesting meaty conversation that at least I was hoping would follow. I

balked for a moment, but came up with a reasonably interesting question to get a conversation started. Just as she was into her response in came the disastrous bomb. The bomb was one of her married female friends. She butted into our conversation without invitation. "Oh hi, Rachael! How is your bible study going? I'm sure it's going well. Did you get a chance to......BLAH....BLAH...BLAH......" At that point all I heard from this married lady's mouth was "Me, me, me. It's all about me. I don't care if you are standing there about to make a connection with Mr. Eligible. I want to talk to you NOW. My relationship with you is much more significant than his relationship with you." And on and on.

What was equally annoying was that Mrs. Married didn't even bother to look at me, say, "Excuse me," or "I'm sorry to butt in, but I really have to talk to Rachael right now. By the way my name is Rosy." Nothing! These inconsiderate friends, be they married or single, will devastate your chances of making a meaningful connection with Mr. Eligible. Of course they can still be your friends. I recommend, however, that you come up with a pithy phrase that you can utter to them when you don't want to talk to them at that moment. Here's a suggestion for a pithy phrase. This short scene was inspired by a skit with Chris Farley on *Saturday Night Live*. Here's the skit on YouTube. http://www.youtube.com search 9YfvBbxE1vU He was dressed like an overweight woman on a very restricted diet. Now the hungry animal in her broke out to get the food she wanted despite criticism from her friends.

While gently but confidently clutching Mrs. Married's neck with your hand, staring intently into her eyes with a deep growl in your voice walk her slowly backward away from Mr. Eligible and speaking the following words. "Mrs. Married, you know how I've been praying to the Lord for a husband.

And now here you are cutting me off from a man who could potentially be him. Do you enjoy seeing me suffering in this lonely single life because you're really blowing it for me right now? In fact if you don't turn and step away from our moment I will have to take drastic action against you. I'm single and I'm being courted right now and you're standing between my marriage altar and me. Don't mess with my longings." That should make your intentions clear enough. Then turn back to the man with a big smile on your face and in your saccharine sweetest most delicate feminine voice say, "Now where were we?"

For all I know Rachael in the above example used some secret signal to indicate to Mrs. Married to rescue her from having a conversation with me. In fact maybe this entire book is based on my naivety to women's secret signals. If so, this book is about ridding that cancer of secret signaling from the inner workings of women's group interactions.

Maybe you can come up with a pithy phrase of your own that is a wee bit more tactful. How about this one. "Hi Mrs. Married. Mr. Eligible this is Mrs. Married. Mrs. Married can you give us a minute? Mr. Eligible and I need a few more minutes to finish up." If Mrs. Married doesn't know to turn and butt out, then you will have just learned of a possible reason why you are still single. With girl-friends like Mrs. Married, you won't need a chastity belt. As far as Rachael goes I was equally annoyed with her and Mrs. Married. She didn't have the spine to handle Mrs. Married. Rachael would rather kiss up to Mrs. Married than further her own possibilities of marriage with Mr. Eligible. In my opinion Rachael has a character issue. Sometimes it's just necessary to risk saying something that could be taken as not so nice. To me there is a character issue when a woman would rather maintain a "nice" reputation with a friend instead of rightfully taking deliberate corrective action with that friend's interfering behavior. In summary be prepared to ward off people who want to cut in on your conversations with Mr. Eligible.

Discuss your private issues anywhere other than at group meetings. But what if Mrs. Married had an urgent and necessary issue to discuss with Rachael? Should I still expect Rachael to put her at bay for four or five minutes to continue talking with me? CERTAINLY NOT!!! An emergency with another sister in Christ is an emergency for me as well. While I may not be able to help Mrs. Married with her issue I can happily "release" Rachael from our conversation so she can console Mrs. Married. I can also pray for Mrs. Married even if I'm not privy to the conversation.

With that said I have to ask you one question. What issue arose in Mrs. Married during the two-hour service that did not exist before arriving at the church service that day? Probably none. Her issue probably existed well before the service. However, Mrs. Married opted to use the church service as a meeting ground with you to selfishly handle her very personal issue.

Is a crowded church lobby abuzz with happy conversation the best place to discuss personal issues? Probably not. Could Mrs. Married have contacted Rachael privately before the service to discuss her issue? Probably. Maybe Mrs. Married's issue was not so urgent after all; she was just being selfish at Rachael and Mr. Eligible's expense.

I call Mrs. Married's behavior CONVERSA-TIONAL GRAND-STANDING. That is, most people—women more so than men—are not comfortable standing alone by themselves in a place where everyone else, at least in their imagination, is engaged in conversation. As such they will cut in to be part of a conversation, and the more urgent they make their issue with you, the more justified, and excused, they feel about cutting in. In summary, you can make yourself more available to conversing with Mr. Eligible by leaving issue-heavy topics anywhere else but at church services or singles meetings. You should expect that same thoughtfulness from your friends, as well. This sentiment is not to say that you should never delve beyond the superficial; there is, however, a time and place for everything.

8. Show physical signs of nervousness even if you're not. Twirl your finger in your hair, fidget, and rock back and forth...whatever. If your hair is up in a bun let it flop down and gently stroke it into place with your hand. If your hair is down gently pull it into a ponytail or bun, letting it drop back down anyway. Guys like to watch women adorn themselves in the name of beautifying themselves. It's a sign that she wants to be as attractive as possible for the opposite sex. In essence, you're in the game of pursuit and seduction. Displaying signs of nervousness or adorning yourself makes you vulnerable and your vulnerabilities are what make you attractive, even innocently seductive.

9. This one is complicated, so it's going to be long. If I told you there is one sure-fire thing you can do to be more attractive to men would you do it? Who wouldn't answer yes unless it compromises your character or faith? I have a room full of single men standing behind me. So let me ask their opinion. Men, if there's one thing a woman could do to attract a man what would it be? And with out any delay or discussion they all respond in unison, "Lose weight!" I'm not suggesting unhealthy weight loss. Here's a link that charts healthy weight per height. Now I can't keep you from concluding that I'm promoting anorexia. I'm not. I'm promoting healthy standards as reported by the scientific community. There is an increasing prevalence of type 2 diabetes (lifestyle-induced) in this country. Hence, an ounce of prevention (exercise and diet

control) shows that you have a wealth of wisdom for the benefit not only of your own future with your spouse but also more immediately for any children placed in your care by the Lord. This advice is as true for men as it is for women. Why would anyone knowingly marry someone with sure signs of avoidable future blindness, loss of limb if not premature death due to a lack of self-discipline in the realm of diet and exercise?

Sorry. I know how harsh "lose weight" sounds. In fairness I should say to my male readers that if you want to make yourself more attractive to women, work out! Sculpt those six-pack abs, pump up your chest and arms, forge those buns of steel. In other words, for both men and women maintain a healthy appearance. On this topic one female Christian author writes: "I know what it's like to get older and find your own body thwarting your efforts to exercise or your metabolism flat-lining. But men appreciate *some* effort being made. They notice a woman who takes the right kind of pride in her appearance, who wants to be womanly. You don't have to be perfect but feminine is good." (McCulley, Carolyn. *Did I Kiss Marriage Goodbye?* Wheaton, Illinois: Crossway Books, 2004) 163.

I did a Google search with the terms "body height and weight chart". Of the options I clicked on the following link.

http://www.disabled-world.com/artman/publish/height_weight.shtml

Check out 3 or 4 different sites with charts to get a good average of body weight recommendation per your height. Michelle Obama, the First Lady to our President is working on a book to be titled, "American Grown". No doubt it will cover childhood obesity since her goal as first lady is to eradicate childhood obesity.

It's sad that the mere mention of checking your weight raises a red flag above my name and Christian character. What about a red flag over parents who fail to teach their children the importance of good diet and exercise habits? What about insults from classmates and kids in the neighborhood that will leave an indelible mark on an obese kid's self esteem? What about health care costs and potential disabilities associated with obesity into adulthood? Are parents helping or actually hurting their child by loving them, "no matter what"? What about adult obesity and attracting a mate? True love for a child is teaching good exercise and diet habits that will last a healthy lifetime hopefully with a mate.

But if you are insulted by the suggestion to lose weight, then go to your next Christian singles group meeting and bunch up with your gender to cry about it. The reality is that both men and women like healthy figures on the opposite sex. This one physical aspect of our being is admittedly ephemeral and superficial but nevertheless effective for attracting the opposite sex. If you insist that you are beautiful the way God made you—and you would be right— then I recommend that you exercise these hints on men who are of the same body type as yours. Just don't complain if you only seem to be able to attract out-of-shape men who say, "I am beautiful the way God made me." It's true for both sexes. But don't be so naive. If you use that excuse for being out of shape, most people, Christian or not, will simply be thinking, "No, you're lazy and undisciplined and that's NOT how God made you."

I'm reminded of a single, out-of-shape woman I got to know. She said that she wants her man to be attracted to her character and personality, not her figure. She said it with such conviction that she seemed to be saying that she keeps herself out of shape just to repel any man who might be attracted to her by her figure alone. Of course men know that a solid relationship of life-long compatibility is built on character and not on figure. That special feeling of attraction to physical beauty in the opposite sex, however, is what motivates us men to pursue one woman among hundreds that are single. So don't knock it. Besides God created physical beauty and men's response to it. So enjoy it.

My out of shape friend was probably harboring feelings of resentment to well-figured men who wouldn't take the time to get to know her for her character. What do you suppose the likelihood is that she similarly rejects out-of-shape men based on their body type without first getting to know their character? What's good for the goose should be good for the gander too.

Physical shape goes hand-in-hand with general appearance. Are your clothes worn out or trendy from a previous generation? Do your clothes naturally say, "I'M A WOMAN!!!!" or do you don sweat suits or hospital scrubs all the time? Or worse, do you wear your power business suit from work? Some women can actually make them look good, but can you? I don't suggest that you go out and turn your wardrobe over every year to keep up with the current trends. Personally that would turn me off even more than wearing sweats all the time. You know how to bargain shop, even finding a perfect clothing article in a secondhand shop.

I took a friend Molly to my favorite local "secondhand rose" shop. I was browsing in the electronics department while she headed for the dresses. I followed her there curious to watch her facial expressions as she pulled dresses off the rack. Would she make snobby disgusted faces or would she see the life that she could breath into a dress just with her being? She asked my opinion every once in a while and she ended up taking three dresses into the fitting room. I wrote her a poem for her birthday later that year. Here is one line that I included: "You can try on a dress costing not much more than a dollar; walking out of the fitting room, you make all the men holler!" Which brings me to another point. Molly has something about her that exudes an inner cheerful attitude. It starts with the smile on her face, eye contact, and her unforced lively walk. It's really hard to say what it is about her. Men are unusually drawn to her based on the number of unsolicited approaches she gets from them. Finally, have you done anything with your hair in this decade? Time for a new wave or cut?

If you go to all the trouble to get fit, put on some makeup, buy a dress, change your hair, etc. . . . and sit in the corner of a room with a blank expression on your face, you might as well volunteer as an historical figure in your local wax museum. Unless you allow yourself to smile, make eye contact, respond in conversation, be of cheerful attitude, etc., you will get more of a response from a "man" in the wax museum. And those things I just mentioned don't cost a penny and never go out of style. God gave them to you for free. Are you currently burying them under a bushel? So while you are slowly getting fit you can take immediate action on improving other aspects of your appearance (smile, eye contact, conversation, cheerful attitude etc..).

Let me go back to my out-of-shape friend. I accused her of maintaining her out-of-shape figure in an effort to ward off men who would only be attracted to her if she were in shape. If you are not motivated to get in shape, are you motivated to show men your inner beauty? After all, isn't it your inner beauty that sustains a long-term relationship? What if you are both out of shape and too bitter or proud to "condescend" to smiling, making eye contact, engaging in conversation, and being cheerful in attitude? Well then, not only are you bringing yourself down, but you're also poisoning the auspicious atmosphere of your Christian singles group. In that case I would recommend that you stop attending and instead find a small, women's care group where you can get to the spiritual root of your reluctance to be attractive.

10. Do that thang' with your eyes that you don't do with your friends. Is it called "batting" your eyes? I don't know what you do, but it works.

11. The wedding ring finger: a true story. Here is an example of an anti-hint that I witnessed firsthand by a woman in a Christian singles group. I met her as we arrived at the church to practice a skit for a coffee house; the singles ministry was sponsoring it. There were six others who would arrive shortly after us to practice with us. As Shellie and I were chatting waiting for the others, I noticed right away that she had an engagement ring on her wedding ring finger. I had not met her before, as she was new to the group. She was about twenty-five at that time. I immediately asked her.

"Are you engaged?" Pointing at her ring.

"No," she replied with a bit of an attitude.

"Are you aware that the custom in this country is for an engaged woman to wear her rock on that finger?"

"Yes," she replied with the same short stop-talking-to-me-about-it attitude.

"Why don't you wear it on a different finger?"

"Because I like it on *this* finger."

"Well, you know, most single guys when they first meet a woman look at her wedding ring finger to see if she's already taken."

"Well then, this ring wards off the kind of guys who are only interested in getting a date with me. If a guy is interested enough in getting to know me, he will not be deterred by the ring."

At that point the dialogue was over because I was pretty much dumbstruck by her bizarre rationale. A few months later it hit me like a ton of bricks the implications of her rationale. The kind of guy she would attract would not be those guys interested in getting to know her as a fellow sister in Christ. In general, guys who persist after seeing the ring have the motivation of ADULTERY!!!!

So the point of this story is if you're single DON'T WEAR RINGS ON YOUR WEDDING RING FINGER!!!! That strategy of wearing one might work well in nightclubs, bars, and business trips, but it's a serious repellant to potential Christian husbands when worn in church, your Christian singles group, or related activities.

12. Watch how QVC models present jewelry such as a choker. I assure you that whatever birthstone or gem dangles from its front and center position is of no consequence to men. It just gives us an excuse to focus on your beautiful neck. If you catch him looking at your neck for too long he will try and save face by saying, "Wow! What kind of birthstone is that? It's lovely". Watch how the model angles her head and neck to showcase the necklace area. Can you sneak one of those subtle movements in while talking to Mr. Right? Do you think that's silly? What's actually silly is that we men will actually be trying to have a coherent conversation with you while trying to peel our eyes off your neck. If showcasing your neck in this way is beyond your Christian conviction of decency I'm not surprised. This body language definitely flirts with the boundary of eroticism. If you have any doubt about it take Hollywood romance movies for example. I don't remember where or when I heard it but during kissing scenes a woman does not have her face directed towards the ground. She is usually looking face up with head tilted back. This position exposes her neck to the viewers adding to the passion of the scene. It adds to her aura of sweet surrender to her Mr. Right. Facing down prevents two things: first, the viewer can't see her neck and second, it causes a bunching

up of her skin in the neck area masking all the naturally attractive and vulnerable contours of her neck. If you are reluctant to go to this extreme to attract a man than just go to this extreme for a good laugh as you watch the man try to maintain composure in your presence. No. I take that back. Don't do it just for a good laugh. That wouldn't be fair to him and you might get yourself into an unwanted pursuit by that man. It really is a powerful hint if you do it artfully.

Is Eye Contact Actually A Hot-Potato Going Back And Forth?

A gal-pal of mine, Sharon, a successful college graduate turned stay-at-home mom wrote the following in response to the topic of eye contact and hint dropping.

"Here's what's even more fun—hold eye contact and SMILE and see what happens. I had a guy yesterday hold eye contact with me, smile, and then wink. Boy, did that send me soaring! He is our Rocco's pizza guy and he always does that to me when I come in. I usually leave not knowing how much I paid for the pizza.

Did you know though that if a girl HAS been making eye contact during conversation and the awkward silence happens, she could be nervous, but there is a flirtatious way she can look away then look back. That indicates to him that she knows he is the dominant one and that she is pleased with that. She might even be blushing when she returns the look. It's the "stare down" and men do it all the time. It must be an alpha male thing. If you are attracted to the guy and he stares at you in admiration, you simply don't know what to do with the rushing feeling you have inside . . . you look away to regain your composure.

On the other hand if I want to let a guy know I'm NOT interested in him, from across the room, I'd wait for us to make eye contact and quickly look away with an aloof tone. I would not give him eye contact for the rest of the night. It sounds mean, but it's a way of saying back off without growling. And I think it's pretty obvious that on a date, if a woman is not smitten she will avert her attention away for long periods of time hinting to him that she's done. She doesn't want to let the conversation linger. She'll also give one-word answers or even bring up topics of conversation that will purposely make herself look unattractive. I've done that before. However, if HE should look away, that is rejection flat out. If he looks away while you're sitting across from each other, THAT'S TERRIBLE even if he does like you. It's incredibly rude.

If you're already friends with him and there is little or no attraction to him and he stares at you, you will respond with, "What's the matter? Do I have something on my face?" And if you're not friends and find him attractive you will look away, look back, blush, giggle, and hope that he breaks the awkward silence. These actions or reactions will happen so naturally; you can't fake or force them. If you want to see if a girl is smitten over you, check her cheeks to see if she is blushing when you stare her down. That gives her true feelings away. Women like alpha males; it makes us feel safe.

But interpreting eye contact can be tricky. If a guy does break eye contact, that *might* be okay, so long he has not focused on something else while he's looking away. If he did focus, that would be an indication to me that "time's up"; he's probably had enough of our exchange, and I'm no longer holding his attention. Some guys, though, do want to continue the time with you. They just have an insulting habit of gazing away or can't control turning their heads to look at another woman or see the score on TV. They may not even be aware of their bad habit. It's pretty rude, though, and you have to decide whether or not it's worth it to you to figure him out.

Women have a sense that indicates when she's captured a man's attention and when he wants more of her. He indicates interest by a sudden scrambling to figure out how he can spend more time with her, stumbling over his words, telling more jokes, trying to keep the conversation going. That's when he is interested or about to ask her for another date, her number, something. It must be very tough on a guy to go through this part of the process—when he knows that the window of opportunity is closing and he has to make a move. I think the standard line is "I had a nice time, can I call you?" Women can sense all of that coming."

THE FOUR-SECOND RULE

I heard this advice recently from a Christian woman given during a singles seminar on dating relationships. A married couple of ten years with two kids did most of the talking. As such I was not surprised when I finally realized that the bulk of their seminar was targeted for Christian singles *already* in some kind of dating relationship. I was not surprised because like most marrieds in the church they are quite clueless when it comes to even vicariously experiencing the "singles scene" even if only in their own church. Indeed, the key observation upon which I wrote this book is that Christian singles are not dating *at all*, never mind the issues that arise with repeat dates with the same person! Anyway at least that married couple was getting singles together for discussion, although I'm positive that no one left there with a date or even a new phone number.

So what's the four-second rule?

The four-second rule is the amount of time a woman should hold eye contact with a man before releasing. This gaze is enough of a hint for a man to pick up on and react *if he is interested*. I agree with her fully. But just as men were once Master Brave as boys (Chapter 14, "MISTER BRAVE

DOESN'T EXIST, BUT MASTER BRAVE DID . . . ONCE") women were once four-second rule experts as girls. And just as rejection checks a boy's bravery into manhood a girl's broken heart checks her eye contact (with Mr. Maybe) into womanhood.

Have you noticed that your eye contact stamina is reduced by a half second with each prospective Mr. Right that breaks your heart? And despite your attraction to Mr. Maybe do you find it physically impossible to so much as look in his direction when you sense that he is looking in yours? If so, you are once bitten, twice-shy, meaning that you were hurt once due to dropping hints (eye contact in this case) and, therefore, subsequent occurrences of eye contact will be avoided. Indeed there is a term for women who can't execute the four-second rule. It is *old maid* or *spinster*! (*Bachelorette* is not included here because it carries with it the essence of a temporary state of being single with a realistic possibility of becoming married.) I have much more to say about eye contact in CHAPTER 16: DON'T OPEN THAT CAN-O-WORMS!

I recently read an interesting article on dating myths. I couldn't find the link when I just checked. The author suggests that when a girl breaks eye contact within the first second of meeting a man's eyes it could mean something I, Eddie B, wasn't expecting. The author continued. A woman knows that her eyes are the unguarded passage to her heart. When a dashing man takes a prolonged look into her eyes she must protect herself from his unwitting manner of seduction by simply averting her eyes from his. It's a defense mechanism that she may not even be aware she's implementing. Avoiding eye contact means preempting impending heartbreak. What do I say to that? Ironically, according to that author's logic, a man that Miss Guarded deems Mr. Awkward poses no threat to her heart and she will allow longer eye contact with him. Sadly, men take prolonged eye contact as a possible hint of her interest. Hence, Miss Guarded wards off men she is attracted to while giving hints to men she is not.

What's my advice? Let Mr. Musing in to your eyes. Let nature take its course. Let your body course through its natural reactions- the blushing, the awkward squirming, the sudden warm surge. Wow! Why deny that natural God-created reaction? Besides, you're a modern day woman; you know how to take care in that situation. Moreover, you should be relatively safe because you will be at church or a Christian singles event with plenty of brothers and sisters around you to keep him and you accountable.

THE BEAUTY OF IT ALL

Do you realize the power of being the hint dropper? In essence you are in control of who asks you out, except for the exceptional guys who don't need hints. If women play their role in dropping hints the onus for a dead dating Christian singles group lies squarely on the shoulders of the men. Wouldn't it be great if you could blame all your stay-at-home Friday and Saturday nights on men? *Of course*! I'm not trying to make a sarcastic point here either.

Can you imagine the introspection that all the men in Christian singles group are going to go through? When they realize that the women have stepped up to their role of hint dropping, men will clearly feel the weight of an expected response on their shoulders. But what if that weight is not heeded and men don't respond in favor of cold feet or indecisiveness? Isn't instilling cold feet or indecisiveness the ultimate revenge that a woman can take on a man, making him think real hard about his disinterest? And the bonus is that you don't have to do anything even remotely complicated to put him in this position! It's beautiful!

How can you now resist getting yourself and your girlfriends to start dropping hints? You have nothing to lose except that a man will ignore your hint. But what you have to gain is one, two, or even three men vying for your attention. Wouldn't that be worth giving hints? If women don't collectively begin to start dropping hints then the men can squarely put the onus of a sterile Christian singles group on women for their apparent reluctance to indulge in God's gift of motivating men in this way. News flash: based on my conversations with men they (we) already *ARE* putting the onus on women.

Remember that old Wendy's commercial slogan, "Where's the beef?" We men are asking, "Where's the hints?"

BUT I DON'T WANT TO FEEL SILLY OR WORSE

You won't feel silly for dropping well-crafted, directed godly, subtle hints. If you follow my hints suggestion list in combination with your own initiatives you will minimize feeling silly. That's the bonus of putting the onus of a sterile Christian singles group on the shoulders of men; men don't know you did it but they, nevertheless, feel accountable for it. Let me explain. Your hint to a man will flash neon signs to him saying ,"BUZZ...ASK ME OUT; I'LL SAY YES. BUZZ...ASK ME OUT; I'LL SAY YES. BUZZ...ASK ME OUT; I'LL SAY YES."

You have fulfilled your role as a woman. He will pick up the hint in kind and ask you out almost immediately, most of the time and usually all the time, but in his time.

In the eyes of an uninterested man, however, your hint will likely pass way over his head. In other words he won't detect your hint. He will stand before you with a blank look on his face and you might feel compelled to poke him in the eye with a stick to see if he is alive. Yet some guys do detect hints even when they are not interested in you. In these two cases what a man will walk away thinking of you is, "Isn't she friendly." That's it!

He will not run off to his circle of friends and giggle about you. Most men just won't do that. Men won't do that because one of his buddies will likely ask, "Oh yeah? Just how do you know she's interested in you?"

And the flattered guy will say, "Well, you know, she kind of moved her shoulders in that......way that....you know....means so much." And of course his buddies will laugh at his presumption based on what appears to be wishful thinking. But that's exactly how your subtle hint should be delivered. It should remain indescribable by the man who receives it.

As such you have little to lose. It would, therefore, be very wise for women to leave their destructive pride packed far away in their apartments, you know, the place where they might be expecting Mr. Musing to come-a-knocking on the door with a marriage proposal. I make this statement because Satan will be at your singles group mocking you saying, "That man just insulted you very deeply by not responding to your hint. You deserve better treatment from men. You would be better off avoiding men altogether. Just wait patiently and do nothing and Jesus will bless you with a husband one day. Yes, Jesus might even send a man directly to your front door, so it's best if you don't attend these meetings or social events at all. Just stay at home and watch soap operas or read Harlequin novels; you'll find real love there."

So you must believe that the status of your pride is not at issue. Remember that you packed it far away to begin with. What you are simply feeling is vulnerability in the face of men. Satan is just trying to turn a beautiful emotional feeling of vulnerability—a gift from God—into the bitterness of destructive pride (an accusation by Satan). Do you see that by being prideful Satan keeps you from dropping more hints and consequently derailing your chances of dating Mr. Right?

Last, I don't know where the phrase "divide and conquer" comes from, maybe Napoleon, but it applies here. One very excellent way that Satan can rid the world of Christians is by dividing the single men from the single women. Obviously they will never marry in this condition and therefore never bear offspring to fill their place in the Church after their death. Indeed, Satan is clever.

If, however, admitting the possibility of interference by Satan is not your cup of spiritual tea, then I offer you the following insight. Of course you will feel vulnerable dropping your hints, but men sensing that vulnerability is what makes them kick into their role as pursuing beings. You simply are unlikely to be wed without dropping your hints. You must decide if the trade-off of showing your vulnerability in exchange for a husband is worth it.

SHE'S JUST BEING FRIENDLY

It has been my experience that some women are naturally predisposed to displaying one or more of the hints I have listed. Moreover, it doesn't take Mr. Right to get them to smile, laugh at corny jokes, maintain eye contact, beat back their female friends while talking to a man, etc. As such it can be a challenge for a guy to know if a woman is dropping him a hint or just being friendly. After all he sees her giving the same "hints" to other guys as well.

I recommend that women just continue being their ole sweet self making an otherwise dull room cheery the moment they step foot into it. If a man founders himself with trying to determine whether or not you're dropping directed hints at him just move on without him. If you really like him you will find a hint to direct toward him that you don't naturally exude to other men. My estimation is that there will be enough guys responding to your natural friendliness that you won't have to be concerned with the men who don't respond. Forget about them; but if you really like a nonresponder, you can figure out a way to register your subtle hint.

One major drawback to having a happy-smiley disposition all the time is that such women will likely be asked out for coffee by many men, even the ones they don't like. You can minimize the impact of this complication by rehearsing the rejection lines I have already written in Chapter 11, JUST SAY IT. You must be well polished in your delivery of these lines in order to not only ward off the Mr. Awkwards but also maintain your rapport with him afterwards. Remember, Mr. Awkward might have a brother or friend that he might introduce to you if your rejection of him is honest and esteeming.

BUT I DO GIVE HINTS, AND MEN STILL DON'T RESPOND

Yes, unfortunately that is the risk of dropping hints. The guy may not respond. In my experience guys can be pretty dumb about detecting hints at the conscious level. It may take a few minutes, hours, days, and even months before he realizes that you've been dropping hints. Women must deal with guys who are just as dumb as doorknobs when it comes to understanding when and if a woman is dropping hints. Sorry, but that's just the way we are.

Here's a great pithy proverb (that I just made up) to help you understand the importance of being persistent at dropping hints. The sooner you accept this fact the sooner you can be an effective hint dropper. "You must sew the seeds of godly, subtle hints before you can reap a man-harvest."

But all men are not hint dense. There are guys who can immediately detect a subtle hint upon its delivery. They know when a woman indicates that she is interested in him. This next sentence is very important and it bears repeating from the above section BUT I DON'T WANT TO FEEL SILLY OR WORSE. If he does not follow up with some kind of pursuit, *he is not interested in you*. Well, at least not interested at that time. You run the risk that he actually detects your hint and is laughing hysterically inside that you should think he would be interested in pursuing you. He could turn around to his buddies and say, "Oh.....my......God! You would not believe who just gave me a subtle hint!" And they would all get a laugh at your expense, right?

Wrong! Guys just don't do that. So you only lose face with the man to whom you direct your hint. Nevertheless, getting no indication of pursuit behavior from him is indeed rejection by him. Ouch! That stings, doesn't it? And that is precisely why I now believe that women have the much more emotionally difficult role of dropping hints. A guy's follow-up to your hint with an invitation out for a date is no risk at all in comparison. He already knows you're going to say yes so there is little to no risk for him.

Your hint is like giving him the option to ask you out or not. Moreover, even if you do say no to him, he'll just quickly dismiss any feelings of rejection he feels by thinking, "Oh, my mistake. I thought she was giving me a hint; I'm such a dense male." Or he could think, "Well, I feel good because if she were giving me a hint, I just did my part as a man by asking her out." Little harm is done and he moves on. However, don't expect him to ask you out again unless you drop an overt hint (subtle hints from you will no longer register on his radar). My recommendation is for you to avoid having to resort to overt hints. Just say yes if Mr. Mistaken asks you out.

CHAPTER 6

INTRODUCING MR. BRAVE

WOMEN'S REBUTTAL

The previous two chapters discuss my hypothesis (women are the initiators of subtle hints) and suggestions for hints. Hands down the unanimous rebuttal from women to my hint dropping suggestion is paraphrased as follows.

"It's not my job to give off hints even if subtle. If a man is interested in me he will approach me no matter what. That's *his* job. *He* must initiate the date because *he* will be the leader should we marry and raise a family. If he fails to demonstrate leadership at initiating a date I doubt he will demonstrate leadership in a marriage."

If that is also your argument against subtle hint dropping the rest of this chapter will give you something to think about regarding the man's role in initiating a date with you.

COLD-TURKEY

Mr. Brave is what I call a man stepping out cold-turkey to express his interest in a woman. "Cold-turkey" because he has no idea or even any hint from her that she would be even vaguely receptive to his advance. I'm not sure when or how the term cold-turkey originated. Maybe the man is the turkey and the woman is cold. Nevertheless, such men have incredible self-confidence and an unusual drive to overcome (or at least repress for a minute or two) his fear of rejection. Indeed, this is the kind of man that God hopes to form through intense study of Holy Scripture. Suffice it to say that we are a fallen race and having that Holy Scripture faith is virtually impossible without the help of the Holy Spirit and a lot of time dedicated to sanctification.

So please remove us men from that pedestal in favor of the reality that we men in our twenties, thirties, and forties are saved sinners with a lot of sanctification to go. Mr. Brave also has the resolve to hold his head up high after getting 9 rejections out of 10 invitations.

Here's an anecdote from a sitcom episode of Seinfeld. ("The Lip Reader." Seinfeld. Sienfeld, Jerry and Larry David. NBC. 1993). It encapsulates what men suffer before asking out a woman cold-turkey. George and Jerry were enjoying a tennis match when Jerry noticed how beautiful the woman line judge was.

> George: Boy you are really smitten.
> Jerry: I gotta talk to her. What do you think?
> George: Cold? How are you going to do that? You're not one of those guys.
> Jerry: I'm going to psyche myself into it like those people that just walk across the hot coals.
> George: They're not mocked and humiliated when they get to the other side.
> Jerry: I have to. I won't be able to live with myself.
> George: Wait a minute Jerry, there's a bigger issue here. If you go through that wall and become one of those guys I'll be left here on this side. Take me with you.
> Jerry: I can't.
> George: What are you going to say?
> Jerry: I don't know, "Hi".
> George: You think you're going to the other side with "Hi"? You're not going to make it.

That anecdote emphasizes the unlikelihood that a guy will ask a woman out cold-turkey, unless of course, she is a super-model or extremely desirable. Most women are neither, so you might reconsider having a "sit back and let the men approach me uninvited" disposition. Moreover, if you are truly convinced that a man should approach you uninvited, then by logical extension any man who does so measures up to some of your basic criteria of your future mate. You have to be careful, though.

Once men learn that a woman expects men to ask her out cold-turkey, she will get a variety of men (being gentle with my use of "variety" to describe them) approaching her uninvited (cold-turkey) to ask her out. On a practical note, it may take time for the men in your group to learn this aspect about you. Some men may never learn it. Some will not approach women cold-turkey anyway.

Are you willing to wait on establishing a reputation that may never become known and furthermore, may never become known to the men by whom you actually want to be asked out? You may have to suffer through a variety of men's invitations until you receive one from a guy to whom you are even vaguely attracted. The reality is likely that you are *not* open to invitations from any ol' Mr. Brave, no matter how confident he was in asking you out cold-turkey. And it only takes a handful of men to be rejected by you before you get the counterproductive reputation of being a cold-hearted woman. Then it is *really* unlikely that Mr. Right will ask you out cold-turkey.

Do you now understand how dropping hints avoids hurt feelings and awkward moments in your singles group? A well-crafted hint is enough to motivate him to action, unless of course he is not mutually interested in you or he simply has no radar to detect your hint. If he is worth it to you then you may have to be persistent or drop a slightly less subtle hint. But be fully convinced that it would be a mistake to cross the line between a subtle hint and outright asking him out.

HE'S MR. BRAVE BUT CAN HE LEARN?

Some define craziness as trying the same thing over and over again getting the same unwanted result but expecting something different to happen the next time. In the lab as a Ph.D. student I *had* to think like a crazy person. Lucky for me that each failed experiment I repeated eventually *did* give a successful result. I would definitely *not* apply the same tactic to asking out women who are not hinting to me. I hope the following section will alert you to possible drawbacks of waiting only for Mr. Brave to ask you out cold-turkey.

Humans have the wonderful and unique capacity to learn and to pass on that knowledge to others and subsequent generations. Learning does not occur by making repeated attempts like a crazy person. Depending on the task at hand a man will try the same approach two, three, four, or even ten times. But he will eventually learn what doesn't work and try something else.

When you finally marry a man you will be thankful that he learns quickly how to correctly approach marital issues, keep you comfortable, put the toilet seat down, etc. He can adapt. Thus a learning man is to everyone's advantage, especially yours when he is your husband. Yet in order to ask a woman out, Mr. Brave ignores his previous rejections or failures before asking a new woman out.

A typical man's date invitation is very difficult emotionally because he is not a crazy person who doesn't mind doing the same wrong thing over and over again. But to get a date with you he will, in summary, act like a crazy person in his expectation of getting a different result—an acceptance for a date. In every other aspect of his life he will not act like a crazy person. So tell me. Are you a Miss America humdinger of a beauty queen that a guy will go against what he learned—a non-hinting woman will reject his offer for coffee—and act like a crazy person to risk asking you out?

Are you beginning to get a clearer picture of the incredible fortitude you are expecting from a man to ask you out when you are not giving him any hints of interest? Such Mr. Braves are exceptional but they do exist. You can continue to keep your non-hinting posture around the guy you desire to get to know, or you can add a small pinch of catalyst hint to ignite a potentially electrifying reaction. What do you have to lose but your foolish pride and your time-untested approach to meeting Mr. Right? Actually, your approach may be time-tested to be a failure since you are reading this book.

If you are still not convinced to change your ways, I offer the following. Mr. Brave is out there, even though he is exceptional. You have to look in the mirror and ask yourself, "Am I so exceptional that I will attract Mr. Brave uninvited?" I don't doubt for a second that you just might be exceptional in your beauty. God certainly thinks so. So do your family members. Given the right timing and exposure to meeting single men you will probably be asked out by Mr. Brave, cold-turkey. You had better be right, though, about your exceptional self-evaluation or you'll be old, alone and bitter before you know it.

How can you be sure that Mr. Brave is not, after all, just plain crazy for pursuing you without a hint? He is either a self-confident and persistent true go-getter in all aspects of his life or he is simply obsessed with getting a date with women like you who are out of his "league". He asks out such women cold-turkey never meeting with a "yes" and only succeeds in making them feel awkward. For your sake, I hope you can discern the difference between healthy persistence and menacing obsession.

MEN CHANGE THEIR APPROACH

Hollywood romanticizes male persistence in winning his beauty queen. But when does this type of undaunted male pursuit behavior put women at a disadvantage? Here's a practical example.

Neanderthal man tries to start a fire to cook dinner and keep his family warm. He reaches up for a green branch on the nearest tree. He tries for hours to get it to flame up, but because this wood is wet with water it's not going to burn.

He then grabs a green branch recently knocked off a tree by a passing dinosaur. He thinks," Green like first branch but it not on tree." He tries for hours to get it to flame up, but it won't because this wood is still wet despite being found on the ground.

Neanderthal man next tries to light a brown dead piece of wood he pulled from the soggy ground. It doesn't light despite the fact that it's a brown dead piece of wood. He goes on and on trying wood in different condition until finally he tries to light a dead piece of wood that he found perched atop a dry rock baking in the sun. With minimal effort the wood lights up. He says, "Dead and dry wood good."

All the while his Neanderthal wife and kids are waiting in the cave for dinner. They hope that next time they need a fire Poppa Neanderthal will remember what kind of wood worked to get a fire ablaze and dinner on the dirt floor before they become extinct.

WHEN PERSISTENCE BECOMES OBSESSION

We men are like Poppa Neanderthal; we try this and that, and if it doesn't work or give us the desired outcome we change our strategy. Mrs. Neanderthal is thankful that Poppa Neanderthal changed his fire-making strategy instead of obsessing on figuring out how to make green branches burn.

If asking women out cold-turkey nets the man rejection let's say four out of four times a non-crazy man will change his strategy. He might learn to observe subtleties in the women's behavior toward him as a means of pre-measuring success probability of getting a "yes" from a woman. I admit that maybe I'm simply justifying my own cowardliness on the issue of asking a woman out cold-turkey. But let me remind you again of one definition of a crazy person. A crazy person tries the same thing over and over again getting the same unwanted result but expecting something different to happen the next time.

I suspect that Mr. Brave might also be of the persistent attitude that "it's my way or the highway" or "my way is always right". Mr. Brave might be quite successful at his career and taking care of your physical needs. But will he be able to argue with you in a fare and non-dismissing manner and willing to compromise with you when necessary?

Untitled For A Reason

This section illustrates several good points. In some sense it's a recapitulation of the following themes: men's fear of rejection, Mr. Brave's obsession, women's insistence on cold-turkey approaches and women's lack of esteeming rejection skills. By the end of this section you will see how women's subtle hints take the awkwardness out of a date invitation for both men and women.

Mr. Brave has found the apple of his eye. She has no clue yet that he is interested. She doesn't even know he exists. As such it is impossible for her to drop hints to him even if she were interested. Let's call her Miss Indifferent.

Mr. Brave is undaunted by Miss Indifferent; he approaches her against his childhood reservations. He strikes up a conversation and Miss Indifferent responds minimally with yes/no answers never reflecting questions back to him. Mr. Brave persists. The next time they are at the Christian singles group he makes a beeline to her for more conversation or more accurately for more monologue with her. She is somewhat annoyed that he is taking her time when she could be meeting that other guy, Mr. Musing, if he were to show up.

The following Sunday Mr. Brave sits next to her at service. Now Miss Indifferent is fully aware of Mr. Brave's interest in her. Despite her lack of chemistry or interest for him she is nonetheless flattered by his pursuit. However, she still displays indifference to him. In Christian singles group outings, Mr. Brave carpools in the same car with her, asks her to dance, invites her to skate together during the couples only songs, sits across from her in group lunches at Chili's, etc. Indeed, the other men in the Christian singles group recognize Mr. Brave's interest in Miss Indifferent and sit back in envy of his boldness.

All of this pursuit behavior starts to grow on Miss Indifferent; she even starts to subconsciously look forward to seeing what Mr. Brave is going to do next. Her body language, however, still displays indifference to him. Mr. Brave persists. Through the course of several weeks he gets to know more and more of her background and interests. He even presents harmless tokens of his interest like a postcard from a place they both visited at different times with the group, an attractive small stone to remind her of a hike their Christian singles group took together, a paperback book that they talked about in conversation, etc.

After three months of building such a rapport Miss Indifferent begins to wonder if he will ever ask her out on a date. But she continues to show indifference, since she expects brave pursuit behavior from her imagined Mr. Musing. Finally Mr. Brave calls and arranges with her to drop off a popular worship CD at her house. He arrives at the appointed time, gives her the CD, and they chat for a spell on the front porch swing. He finally musters the courage to ask her out, and she reluctantly accepts.

After their date Miss Indifferent is still...indifferent, while Mr. Brave steps up his pursuit mode only guessing that he has a foot in the door with her. The long and short of it is that Miss Indifferent warms up to Mr. Brave, and she falls in love with him. They are now engaged with wedding plans coming along without any hitches. This end result is what I suspect non-hinting women dream about. She feels pursued and that does something for her attraction for Mr. Brave.

Now let's look at another example. No it's not different behavior from Mr. Brave; in fact, his behavior is a carbon copy of the Mr. Brave described above. The only aspect of the story that is different is the behavior of Miss Indifferent. No, you will not be reading an accidental copy and paste of the same story; it was copied and pasted for a reason. Read on and be alert to the subtle differences in Miss Indifferent's reaction to Mr. Brave.

Mr. Brave has found the apple of his eye. She has no clue, however, that he is interested. In fact she doesn't even know he exists. As such it is impossible for her to drop hints to him even if she were interested. Let's call her Miss Not-interested.

Mr. Brave is undaunted by Miss Not-interested; he approaches her against his childhood reservations. He strikes up a conversation and Miss Not-interested, responds minimally with yes/no answers never reflecting questions back to him. Mr. Brave persists. The next time they are at the Christian singles group he makes a beeline to her for more conversation. She is somewhat annoyed that he is taking her time when she could be meeting that other guy, Mr. Right Across-the-Room.

The following Sunday Mr. Brave sits next to her at service. Now Miss Not-interested is fully aware of Mr. Brave's interest in her. She is annoyed that Mr. Brave is going to expect an answer when he asks her out for coffee or whatever annoying event he has in his mind for them. She shares this recent development with her gal-pals who commiserate with her on the burden of having to reject Mr. Brave.

She feels no attraction or interest for Mr. Brave, and she is increasingly disturbed by his further pursuits. Meanwhile the expression on her face is indifferent toward Mr. Brave's attention. In Christian singles group outings, Mr. Brave carpools in the same car with her, asks her to dance, invites her to skate together during the couples only songs, sits across from her in group lunches at Chili's, etc. With each encounter with Mr. Brave, Miss Not-interested becomes increasingly annoyed.

Afterward, Miss Not-interested bunches up with her girlfriends to ridicule and laugh about Mr. Brave's naivety and how "out of her league" he is.

All of this pursuit behavior greatly disturbs Miss Not-interested; she even overtly worries about what he's going to do next. Her body language, however, still advertises indifference to him. Mr. Brave persists. Through the course of several weeks he gets to know precious little of her background and interests because conversing with her is like pulling teeth. Mr. Brave even presents harmless tokens of his interest in her like a postcard from a place they both visited at different times in their lives, an attractive small stone to remind her of a hike their Christian singles group took together, a paperback book that they talked about in conversation, etc.

After a few weeks Miss Not-interested starts to realize that Mr. Brave is not going to give up. But she continues to avoid having a frank conversation with Mr. Brave about how his pursuits are making her very uncomfortable. Finally Mr. Brave calls and arranges with her to drop off a popular worship CD at her house. Now she's freaking out thinking that he's going to start visiting her at home. She immediately calls two girlfriends desperate for advice and gossip. He arrives at the appointed time to deliver the CD, and as she hangs up the phone she wonders if she will eventually have to report his behavior to a brother in leadership in the Christian singles group or perhaps an elder in the church.

They chat for a spell on the porch swing, but that night she has a nightmare that Mr. Brave's behavior turns into a relentless stalker. The advice of her women friends is for Miss Not-interested to finally and convincingly tell Mr. Brave to "cease and desist" or the matter will be taken before the church authority and if necessary the local police authority.

The following week Miss Not-interested has the fateful conversation with Mr. Brave. Mr. Brave realizes that to her he has all along been Mr. Wrong. Needless to say Mr. Wrong is devastated by Miss Not-interested's confession that she is not in the least interested in him and, in fact, was beginning to feel stalked by him. No, Mr. Wrong is not devastated by being rejected by Miss Not-interested; he is actually suffering inner turmoil over the fact that his pursuits led Miss Not-interested to extreme mental duress.

The take-home message is that while Mr. Brave/Wrong behavior was essentially the same in the cases of Miss Indifferent and Miss Not-interested it was the woman's level of receptiveness that differed. Unfortunately for Mr. Wrong, he may now have an undeserved reputation as being romantically out of touch with reality.

Now what are Mr. Wrong's chances of getting a date in that group? He lost the girl he was pursuing, he lost the girls in whom Miss Not-interested confided and he gained an unfavorable reputation. How would you like that as a consolation prize for pursing a woman cold-turkey? Needless to say this hypothetical scenario might just explain why men are not as forthright as they could be when it comes to pursuing women in a manner that used to be courageous and honorable (i.e.,

cold-turkey, no hinting behavior required from the woman).
Do you blame us?

Do you suppose that such an encounter with Mr. Wrong
will be long forgotten in a day or two by Miss Not-interested?
Probably not. As a woman she will evaluate Mr. Wrong's
approaches and her responses to them. She will then make
changes to better handle the next Mr. Wrong who may
approach her. The thing is that Miss Not-interested will also
be on guard even when Mr. Right steps up to her. In physiological lingo she has been sensitized by her experience with
Mr. Wrong. That is to say that Miss Not-interested/ Sensitized
will err on the side of safety, even perhaps unwittingly putting
off repulsive body language when Mr. Right steps up to her
plate. She wants to avoid a repeat of the nightmare with Mr.
Wrong.

Sadly Mr. Right is the one the Lord has set aside for Miss
Not-interested/ Sensitized. But he's not Mr. Musing so her
body language will likely send him away. Women don't have
much choice in the body language that they exude; it's a subconscious thing over which there is little control. This conclusion may paint a dim picture. As such it is my prayer that you
avoid becoming sensitized by Mr. Wrongs in the first place.
You can avoid accretion of repulsive body language by being
forthright in your communications with Mr. Wrongs. Do you
see how being forthright saves Mr. Wrong, you, and your
friends from unprofitable investment of time and gossip?
Everybody wins.

Now do you understand a little better why most guys will
not pursue a woman cold-turkey? I originally wanted to call
this section "Dr. Romantic versus Mr. Stalker," but I was
afraid that it would minimize the effect of presenting the two
scenarios one after the other without giving the point away by
the title. This section is a play on the novel, "Dr. Jeckle as Mr.
Hyde." The main difference is that it is the woman's point of
view (or level of chemistry) that makes a guy out to be Dr.
Romantic or Mr. Stalker, *not* what the guy does or doesn't do.

I'VE BEEN SCOOPED

At this point I ask you, and please be honest with yourself, do you really want men to be as forthright as to ask you out on a date with no given hint of interest from you in the first place? Just remember if you answer yes to that question, you must be ready to entertain invitations from ten Mr. Wrongs for every one Mr. Musing that comes along. Are you sure you're forthright and honest enough to handle rejecting the numerous Mr. Wrongs? Remember by rejecting Mr. Wrong with honesty and dignity he might just be the one to introduce you to Mr. Right.

The last section dealt with the concept that the same pursuit behavior by a man for you can be interpreted in two ways, depending on your level of attraction for him. If you feel no attraction, he is a stalker; if you are attracted to him, he is Mr. Musing. It's all based, not on his behavior, but on your level of attraction for him. This concept was cleverly portrayed in a skit on *Saturday Night Live* on April 16, 2005. To my credit I wrote about this concept well before that skit aired (you can view it at http://www.youtube.com search gBVuAGFcGKY or search Tom Brady on SNL skit (Smigel): "Sexual Harassment and You"

In brief the skit showed the approach of two men for the same co-worker woman at different times. The first man was dressed up to be a geek, dork, and Mr. Bore all wrapped up in one person. The second was the quarterback Tom Brady from the Super Bowl-winning New England Patriots. The same woman reacted completely different to the advances of the two men despite the fact that the two men did nothing different in their approach. Well, sort of. Read on.

In response to the dorky guy the woman was already on the phone with security simply because he looked at her "in that way" as he walked up to her office cubical to ask her out. In contrast her reaction to Tom Brady was warm and inviting to put it mildly. To ram the point home Tom Brady was actually dressed in nothing more than a shirt, tie, and boxer shorts! Despite his unacceptable lack of clothing, the woman was nonetheless fawning over him, even volunteering her home phone number which Tom stuffs into his boxer shorts. She was floating on Cloud Nine with passionate feelings of romance and delight despite his bizarre and totally unacceptable approach. The commentator at the end of the skit says something like, "So if you want to ask somebody out at work, be handsome, be attractive, and don't be unattractive."

So what's the point of this section? Giving no hints to a man when you actually want him to pursue you sends men a statement. The statement is that *all* non-hinting behavior displayed by a woman might not mean lack of interest in a man. We men, therefore, won't know the difference between your interest or lack thereof until you either fall in love with us or file a restraining order against us.

Let me emphasize that whether a man is Dr. Romantic or Mr. Stalker has nothing to do with his behavior but whether or not *you* are interested in his pursuits. Nevertheless to avoid the risk of unfairly being labeled a Mr. Stalker, some men will simply turn to a much less desirable woman who does give him a hint of interest. Other men will simply opt for singleness rather than marry a hinting woman for whom he feels no chemistry. I propose that Christian singles groups are chuck-full of men in the latter category. They won't pursue a hinting woman for whom they feel no chemistry but they also won't approach a non-hinting woman for whom they do feel chemistry.

A frenzy of dating activity is on the verge of eruption in your Christian singles group. The only reactant missing is not a reactant at all; it's what in chemistry is called the activation energy or the catalyst to kick-start the eruption. And the onus of whether or not the reaction starts sits squarely on the women's shoulders. The catalyst is your hint. What will you do with your catalyst? Are you going to hide it under a bushel, or are you going to let it shine?

To conclude, a guy will be reluctant to pursue a non-hinting woman for fear of not only rejection but also for fear of causing emotional torment in an uninterested woman. A hint from you pretty much minimizes both fears. Is that too much to ask in a politically correct culture where men have been beaten down into submission of the new and often times elusive behavioral expectations?

I had a really bad experience once. Admittedly my naive pursuit behavior legitimately unsettled the woman. I sent her a couple of friendly anonymous letters through the mail. I did not even reveal myself while working at the computer help office where she worked. I finally got the nerve up to introduce myself to her there. Her jaw dropped and immediately scolded me over tainting her life with fear of a stalker. That night I didn't sleep well.

Late in the night I woke up with the overwhelming sensation of the presence of Satan in my bedroom. Through my bedroom window the streetlights shining through the bare tree branches cast moving shadows across my bedroom floor and walls. My vulnerable and receptive mind saw images of evil demons taunting me and laughing at me for having caused such horror in the mind of a woman I adored. I vowed that night that I would never cause a woman that kind of mental distress again. Obviously I have learned since then what is appropriate and acceptable pursuit behavior.

But the residue of that nightmare tends to make me err on the side of engaging in no pursuit behavior at all rather than risk freaking out another woman. I have honestly joked these past two or three years that I become more and more reluctant to ask out women cold-turkey even when I think I'm getting a hint because, "I just can't handle seeing not even one more time even just a hint of that expression of terror spread across her face when I ask her out."

Have you ever seen the painting *The Scream* (http://www.flickr.com/photos/oddsock/100761143/) *by* Edvard Munch, 1893)? So now you know what the haggard old woman on the bridge in that painting just experienced. She's reacting to Mr. Wrong's invitation to a date! Now you know a little better what men have to mentally prepare for upon embarking on asking a woman out on a date. It's nice that for women when you drop subtle hints you only get two reactions. First, no reaction at all. Second, an invitation to a date. Seems like minimal mental risk for the potential marriage rewards to which your hint might lead.

CHAPTER 7

TO THINE OWN RATING BE TRUE

DR. EDDIE B'S LAWS OF MINIMIZING REJECTION

Given my bent for scientific solutions, I have a logical and down-to-earth strategy for women to help them decide on whom a hint is dropped. Because we humans fear rejection and/or being ignored, I recommend using the following approach to determine which person to target. My system will increase the likelihood that a man will in turn respond. This system works for both women and men.

This exercise will be a reality check for many readers. You can either do it in your head or you can grab your "who's who" magazines, your high school/college yearbook, and your scissors to make yourself a lasting reminder. (I wish I could be a fly on your wall as you perform this exercise just to watch your expression when you finally determine your number. What kind of resolve or modesty or new confidence will spread across your face?)

Across your bed or other flat surface spread out, left to right, ten eight-and-a-half-by-eleven sheets of paper each labeled with a number, starting with 1 and ending with 10. These numbered pages will make columns across your surface. Now go through your portraits and identify the best looking and worst looking people. Do this selection for two different categories, one for men and one for women. The best looking will be your "10s" and the worst your "1s." Place these pictures below their respective numbered columns. You can have more than one photo per number; just place them below each other in a column so you can see each one.

Now go back and find portraits of people of varying levels of physical attractiveness in between 1 and 10. Assign an attractiveness value to them from 2 to 9. Place the photos under their respective numbered columns. You now have an attractiveness scale of people starting with the least attractive under Column 1 to the left progressing through 2, 3, 4 . . . 8, 9, and 10, the most attractive.

You might be thinking, "Does this guy treat all people simply as numbers on a scale? Where is Christ's love in this picture?" Bear with me; there is a good point that I'm heading for. It's actually a lesson in humility. Besides, I suspect that most people (whether they are willing to admit it or not) make such superficial assessments based on physical appearance.

Go through this rating system for both men and women. Be sure that you rate physical attractiveness only, not personality or character or wealth; that will come next. If you draw a mental block then just rate people on how you think the secular world would rate them.

Now find an average portrait of yourself. Choose a picture of how you typically look at your Christian singles group or church service (i.e., make-up, dress, hairstyle, etc.). Now go to the columns from 1 to 10. Find a place in that scale where your portrait equals the attractiveness of the others. You might think you're more attractive than a 6 but not quite as attractive as a 7. So call yourself a 6.5. Now take your portrait over to the attractiveness scale of the opposite sex. Place it at 6.5 (or whatever you just determined yourself to be). Take a good hard look at the portraits at 6 and 7. If you're a woman these are the men to whom you might consider dropping hints.

On *House, M.D.*, (premiered on Fox Broadcasting Network November 16, 2004) one episode (gave up trying to determine which one) included a 40-year-old woman on the scale of 9 visiting a 40-year-old male patient on the scale of 6. House went up to her and said, "You must be a coworker or sister." She asked why he didn't guess she was the patient's wife. House replied, "A four marries a four. A seven marries a seven and a nine marries a nine. There's a little wiggle room for women though; but even so, you are way out of his league."

As a general rule a woman can shoot for men one level higher on this scale than what she is, one and a half levels higher at most. For example if you are a woman at 6.5 you can shoot for a man up to 8, max. Of course a woman can shoot for a man any level lower than she is.

A man, on the other hand, should not expect to receive hints from a woman who is half a level or more higher. If you are a man at 7, for example, you should not be holding out for a hint from a woman who is 7.5 or higher.

Notice that these numbers favor the woman catching a man who is more attractive than she is. Why? I don't know but here's a stab at it. Men's sex drive is less patient than a woman's so he will compromise his criteria list sooner than a woman would.

Also, if this book's thesis is correct, men are starving for subtle hints from a woman. A hint from a 6 woman received by a 7.5 man just might be the only sign of interest he's had in months or years. Maybe even an 8 man would respond to her hint. For sure the field of Christian men is ripe for the harvest; women just have to fire up the harvest engine of the soul by dropping hints.

WHAT CAN YOU DO TO INCREASE YOUR SCALE RATING?

I hope you're thinking right now that looks aren't everything when it comes to choosing a mate and that looks are only skin deep. To that I say, congratulations; you've learned this adolescent lesson well. I'm not about to lecture you on how to go beyond the physicality of Mr./Miss Coffee's exterior body. You can get some really good advice from Christian self-help authors for that. But let me give you some pointers on increasing your scale rating. Actually these pointers can only increase your scale rating based on the perception of the opposite sex. That is to say, your looks don't change any by using my pointers, just another's perception of you does. The following tips are offered as ways to increase your scale rating simply by tapping into the talents with which the Lord has blessed you.

1. Get involved with serving and volunteering at your Christian singles group. Positions of leadership and high-profile supporting roles are especially effective at breathing life into your scale rating. This strategy may sound self-serving, and it clearly is. But you will also be serving your Christian singles group simultaneously; it's a win-win situation. Don't knock it. Get involved with giving announcements, join the worship band, be a discussion group leader, host a Bible study/small group, get on the social events planning committee. You've got to peel yourself off the wall, as attractive a wallflower that you might be, and get into action.

2. Take a college course or a night class through your community's adult education program offered through your local high school. If you don't have a college degree, go back to school full-time and get one or finish one. Telling Mr./Miss Maybe that you are taking a class shatters the image that you sit home at night watching the recorded soap operas or sports games that you missed during the day. Whether a man or woman if your job is boring to you and, therefore, boring to talk about, take some classes in preparation for a career or hobby change. Sorry, but if you can tolerate a boring and unstimulating job, it may be easily concluded that you are also boring and uninteresting to be with. Alternatively, you are simply lacking the conviction to make necessary changes in your life. You don't lack the talents; just the conviction. Wealthy people hire a personal fitness trainer for that reason. You can simply express your plan in your accountability group, your personal trainers, so they can keep you motivated.

THE TOADY CHRISTIAN SINGLES GROUP GROUPIE

The scale rating approach to increasing the likelihood of a man's response to your subtle hints works for women wanting to make friends with other women as well. Untouchables—women in the 9 to 10 range—are not likely to hang around and confide in Awkward Annie at 3.

I knew Awkward Annie for about five years while in my Christian singles group. She was a 3. She was constantly talking with women 8 or higher. They treated Awkward Annie nicely in public; she was also a very sweet woman. But Awkward Annie didn't give the same kind of attention to women 7 or below. From my observation she just wanted to ingratiate herself into the Untouchables circle. Men do this, too, but to my "discredit" I never really did. Instead I took my mom's advice and simply sought out people who seemed to be unconnected to any particular circle of attendees. It was a "discredit" to me because I know that had I ingratiated myself into the Untouchable circle of men I probably would have had a much better chance at pairing up with an Untouchable woman.

Paraphrasing my mom's advice, she said that if you want to make friends, find others who are also alone and make your own friendship circle of people. Consequently, my experience of God through *all* people around me has made my life very rich. I guess that is why I would never consider marrying an untouchable woman who only associates with other Untouchables. I'm sure I would find her breadth of life intolerably one-dimensional. However, I would go to great lengths to let her prove herself otherwise.

Following my mom's advice allowed the Holy Spirit to direct my path to men and women to befriend in my singles groups. But because I still have my personal criteria list of Miss Right, I don't see myself becoming attracted to socially awkward women despite growing friendships with them. Nevertheless, I don't know how the Holy Spirit will work through socially awkward people so I will continue to make acquaintances with them.

Admittedly, when I hit my late thirties I started to sever some ties with socially awkward people. I guess I became tired of the "tooth-pulling" dialogues. They require much mental work, creativity, drawing out, and patience that I found myself running short. Perhaps that season of "condescending" has passed on in my life. Now, I just want conversationalists of my equal so I can enjoy them, not drag them out.

I don't know the reason why the Lord put that season in my life; all I know is that I'm a better man for it, even though it is coming to a close. Perhaps this book will draw me into interesting dialogue with all kinds of singles discussing alternative opinions on our common quest for marriage. I would find that very stimulating, at least for a season.

F: How often do you attempt to draw out in conversation the socially awkward in your Christian singles group?

F: Do you feel a wave of fear coursing through your body when Mr. Socially Awkward corners you in conversation?

THEE LIST

We all have a criteria list. The list enumerates the must-haves we require in our future spouse. Whether written down or simply a mental template, we all have a list. By dismissing Mr./Miss Apparently Wrong based on your list you effectively reduce the number of eligible singles in your network. Moreover, you reduce the chance of meeting Mr./Miss Right through Mr./Miss Apparently Wrong. I have more to say about date networking in Chapter 17: GET TO KNOW ME DATES: ADVO-CACY DATING.

Here are some time-tested (value-based) criteria to look for in the a potential marriage partner:

1. Location, location, location. It's as true for finding a spouse as it is for buying a home.
2. Education
3. Religion
4. Socio-economic status (expectation of standard of living)
5. Race (but less and less so with teaching of tolerance)
6. Saver vs. spender
7. Drug user (both legal and illegal) vs. clean living

Here are some not-so-time-tested (attraction-based) criteria:

1. Introvert vs. extrovert
2. Serious vs. humorous
3. Stylish vs. low maintenance
4. BMW vs. Chevrolet
5. Blue eyes vs. brown
6. Square jaw vs rounded
7. Dark hair vs. blond
8. Long hair vs. no hair at all
9. Straight teeth
10. Pouty lips
11. Beard vs. clean shaven
12. Body piercing vs. ear piercing
13. Tattoos vs. character
14. Couch potato vs. hobbyist
15. Dimpled chin vs. cleft chin
16. Artful vs. mechanical
17. Dog vs. cat or no pet at all
18. Husky vs. skinny
19. Tall vs. short

The list goes on and on and, unfortunately, only gets longer as you age. And I have not even broached items in the compatibility category such as disciplined, lazy, ambitious, common sense, controller, nagger, undependable, sexual libido, *cannot set boundaries with meddling parents* etc... That last one is italicized because I just recently added it; it wasn't even on my list when I first wrote this paragraph. And so also *my* list grows with age.

As dear as your criteria list may be to you, a meaningful talk with your favorite married couple will quickly put your list into perspective. The following confession might sound mean, but I used to test the honesty of newlywed couples. In the rare event that two people from my singles group ended up getting married, I would ask them the following question. Did you guys feel chemistry or attraction for each other when you first met? While I've gotten many answers to this question, the universal theme reflected in their faces and body language is awkward reluctance to answer.

That is/was my style of initiating "meaningful talks" with married couples. Older couples tend to be more helpful in getting an answer. Their responses can be lumped into two categories. First, there was initial chemistry that grew quickly but now has simmered down. Second, there was no initial chemistry but attraction grew with getting to know each other. According to the pundits, however, what ultimately keeps two couples together is character and commitment.

Notice that I didn't say that what attracts two people is character and commitment. So I recommend that in addition to the items on your criteria list (I'm not recommending that you throw them away because I don't want to throw mine away either), I recommend that you add "character." You can kind of surmise a person's sense of commitment by observing his character and sense of honesty demonstrated in a variety of life situations. As you start paying attention to character you might start to reorder your criteria list.

F: A man is average in every aspect of physical attraction. However his character is exceptional. Do you accept his invitation for a date?

Here is how I believe women would answer according to age group. If you are eighteen to twenty-five you would probably say, "No, because he's not cool."

If you are twenty-five to thirty you look at him, you look at your list, you look at him, you look at your list. In the back of your mind you hear a barely discernable voice that sizes him up as the donor of half of your children's genes. Of course that voice is ultimately drowned out by the sound of your pencil x-ing through the superficial criteria on your list that he doesn't possess.

If you are thirty to thirty-five you still have the romantic notions of an eighteen- to thirty-year-old, but the voice in the back of your mind is getting clearer and it tells you to risk one date with him just to see if his character or anything unexpected will spark something in you.

If you are thirty-five to forty and you've just finished reading this book you start exuding some hints in his direction and you are happily married in less than a year.

If you are twenty-something and you don't want to end the physical misery of singleness, then stop reading this book immediately. Oh, and if singleness to you is not physically miserable, then why are you reading this book?

CHAPTER 8

ONLINE MATCHING SERVICES

Escape to Internet Dating

When attendees become frustrated with the sterile atmosphere in their Christian singles group, they will likely turn to
worldly secular means to meet their desires. Notice that I
didn't say meet their *needs*. I think we can all live without the
opposite sex. It's true that the human race cannot survive
without the opposite sex, but individual humans can survive
without sex if need be. But what drives us at a deeper level is
a need for passion, romance, companionship, acceptance and
attention from the opposite sex.

Such passion is a strong motivating factor for what we do
and how we behave. If you don't find satisfaction of those
desires in your Christian singles group, you are going to seek
them out elsewhere. Yes, the Lord wants you to find that person with whom you are equally yoked, not only in Him but
also in mutual attraction to your mate. Despite the sterile
atmosphere in singles groups, you are, nevertheless, more
likely to find your mate there than online or anywhere else.

Yet, after several months of attendance in your singles
group you realize that it's probably not going to draw out
your equal on the scale of attraction. So you take matters into
your own hands (fingers) and go online to dating services. You
prefer to avoid handing over your fate to a match made by a
computer program. But don't get me wrong; I agree that this
method for matching people by compatibility is sheer genius.

The only drawback (or advantage) is that it doesn't first match chemistry. Fortunately in your Christian singles group you sense chemistry first with the option of settling compatibility issues later. What this means for online matches, unfortunately, is that you'll simply have to endure countless emails back and forth with Mr./Miss e-Maybe to determine chemistry. I have experienced such countless emailings; they often times petered-out before we actually met.

Indeed, the Internet does connect you with countless singles in any number of selected criteria (i.e. single, Christian, no kids, want kids etc..). But once you select your matches (no doubt based on the feeling of chemistry) from your search a series of emails is initiated to explore further compatibility. After a number of years using online services I decided that emailing for too long actually stifles the matching process. The people involved are either simply not truly motivated to meet (just want some opposite sex attention online) or they get into complicated email dialogues that inevitably pops the balloon of romantic possibility.

For some people these services are a real help. Singles best served by them are those folks attending a fifty-member church located a hundred miles from the nearest general store. Most of the flock is married and they are kind enough to reserve a front pew for you so you can noticeably sit by yourself with plenty of space in case an eligible bachelor happens to blow in the back doors of the church. And then there's bachelor Bob who is constantly grinning and asking you if you want to go out on a date with him or his brother Bob (this name is not a typo; Bob's brother really is named Bob).

Some singles belong to a major metropolitan church with numbers of singles that could easily start up their own self-contained town. (Maybe that's not such a great example to use, since at the low rate that Christian singles are getting married, that town would in one generation become a ghost town.) There are many potential spouses to pursue. Yet many of these folks are also buying into online Christian matching services. This trend or tendency is mind-boggling even though I have tried it myself!

Yet if you are having a difficult time working around the funky dynamics in your metropolitan Christian singles group, it's only natural that you look for a more dating-intentional venue. But just remember that you have a good likelihood of meeting Bob and his brother Bob through it. Some people would say that looking beyond your metropolitan Christian singles group is akin to the mentality that the grass is greener on the other side. I proffer that the grass *could* be very green where you are if only you add the following fertilizer.

Drop godly, subtle hints tailored to specific men that interest you.

Admittedly this fertilizer won't help matters in a singles group that lacks the men you want to attract. But this fertilizer can be applied in your daily walk, not just at church or at the singles group. You can invite men that you attract by your subtle hints to your singles group meetings. Not only will you have a chance to get to know them in a safe environment you also get to introduce them to your church and possibly Christianity for the first time. Nevertheless, if you do head for the Internet you are doing nothing less than advertising your hint, an *E*-hint. Why not try dropping the equivalent hints at your singles group?

THERE'S SAFETY IN ANONYMITY

What attracts so many Christian singles to online matching services? They are both dangerous and safe. They are dangerous because your matches are probably not going to be plugged into your church community and therefore the subscribers on it will have no accountability for their behavior with you. There are many good people out there that don't need accountability to treat you as Jesus commands. Even still, we can be tempted by this lack of community accountability; I know I sure feel that temptation.

But despite all the inherent "dangers" of meeting someone this way, a safe and enjoyable experience can be taken from such services. You just have to proceed with common sense and caution.

So then why are such services also safe? They are safe because each person registered with the service announces electronically that they are interested in finding the right person to marry or, at least, to date for starters. Contrast that electronic announcement with a vocal proclamation made by standing up in the middle of your metropolitan Christian singles group, saying with your most sweetly vulnerable voice (if you're a woman), "I would like to announce that I am interested in finding the right Christian man to marry. Thank you."

Of course that would be the ultimate way to let *all* men know that you are interested in them. But that wouldn't be safe because you are certainly *not* going to be interested in all of them, maybe only five or ten. The rest of the men you would simply have to reject. Who wants to spend a lot of time and energy rejecting men? Moreover, the very men that you are interested in may be turned off by your overt manner of getting the word out.

For men there would be no instinct-driven pursuit satisfaction as a result of responding to your public announcement of your interest in finding a man. Your online matching service has a devised system whereby you make it known that you are relationship-interested. Male members view your participation as a sufficient, but not overt, token of your sincere interest. A man knows that there is plenty of opportunity to pursue you if you are the right person for him and vice versa. In essence this electronic system makes it safe for a woman to announce her interest in finding a relationship without compromising her so called pride or dignity. And it can all be arranged with a few mouse clicks and a credit card.

IT'S PERPLEXING, MIND-BOGGLING AND ENIGMATIC

Many, many Christian men and women go online to various websites to find Mr./ Miss Right. In fact, I hypothesize that Christian women will sooner go out and meet an Internet man than accept an invitation for coffee with regular attendee Fred at her Christian singles group or church.

How much does a woman know about Mr. Internet? A picture? A résumé? A few short essays? Compare that with what she knows about Fred at her singles group. Of course, she probably knows more information about Mr. Internet than she does about Fred. That's because women are selective about who they talk to in Christian singles groups, and besides, if Fred corners a woman into conversation it would be just weird to ask him essay questions such as "How long was your last relationship and why did it end?" The relative anonymity of Internet dating makes such questions tolerable.

Is the dating stagnation within Christian singles' groups a simple matter of "the grass being greener on the Internet side"? Or does the allure of Internet dating give women a better sense that they are in control of their marriage destiny instead of being in the hands of the awkward goofballs in their singles groups? Or is it that women can avoid the role of dropping hints? I have heard it suggested by women that the allure of online dating for women is simply for some attention from a man. She may have little to no intention or interest in actually meeting him, but the e-mail attention she gets from him satisfies her "man fix" temporarily. This misuse of Internet dating is not only sad but it is also terribly degrading to men. Women who misuse internet dating for their temporary "man fix" are no less selfish than men who go online to selfishly use porn for their "women fix".

Getting back to hint dropping, joining an online dating service, of course, is a hint of interest in meeting Mr. Right. However, the hint is not given live and in person so it doesn't really count as a hint. Well, it is a hint only as much as his answers to essay questions and emails reflect who he really is live and in person. That is to say that if he lied about himself in his profile then your hint was given under his false pretense and is thus null and void. Sometimes it's not a matter of people lying but instead a matter of developing an online persona that will never, ever match the live face-to-face persona. Once you meet face-to-face you will ultimately be disappointed that your image of him doesn't match his online persona. By the way his online persona will be based on 50% of what he writes and 50% of how you interpret what he writes.

If you subscribe to an Internet dating site does your online persona match your face-to-face persona, at least the 50% that you can control? I have experienced that what I write online can be very easily misinterpreted by a woman. By not delivering such communications in person, I have no control over how a woman will skew what I write. To be fair, maybe what I interpret to be a woman's misinterpretation of what I write is actually my misinterpretation of her interpretation of what I write. Confused? Indeed, misinterpretations abound in (digital) print.

All that said, I like dabbling in online dating. It's fun, and I get the sense that, in fact, there *are* women out there that might want to date me. This feeling is contrary to the feeling I get from women at my singles' group events. But I wonder who was first to flock to Internet dating, men or women? Did women first stop dropping hints or did men first stop asking women out on dates? It's a modern day version of the old riddle, Which came first, the chicken or the egg?

Since I am a biologist, I do have an answer for the latter question, but it's not the topic of this book.

OPPOSITE EXTREMES OF THE PENDULUM

I like online matching services because they are appearance-based. Admittedly, I am first physically attracted to a woman. But I'm not a Neanderthal; if a physically beautiful woman doesn't posses more long-term compatibility indicators I'll move on. Period. In my profile I am not subtle about this order of importance. Moreover, I advise that the three allowed posted photos be 1) a shot from shoulders up; 2) a full-length shot; and 3) something creative/special. Consequently, I have engaged with a number of women on the topic of physical attraction, one extreme of the pendulum swing.

I argue that physical attraction, stereotypically the male's first motivation, is the *first* thing but surely not *everything* when it comes to finding a mate. Based on women's responses

I would have to say that they stop reading after, "Attraction is the *first* thing.. ." That first half of the sentence typically spirals them into an essay assuring me that 1) physical beauty is superficial; 2) character is internal; 3) no wonder I'm still single; 4) I'll miss out on meeting many spiritually beautiful women; 5) What if my future wife gets pregnant and her body changes? Am I going to have an affair? 6) What if she becomes sick with a condition that leaves her uncontrollably overweight? Am I going to divorce her? 7) What if I do exercise regularly and control my diet, and I still look overweight? Are you going to reject me anyway? 8) You are not a true Christian because physical beauty is too important to you. 9) You need to spend more time in Scripture to become more spiritual.

My follow-up reply to such an unprovoked volley is to ask:

> *"Did you read the whole sentence or just the first half?*
> *I state that attraction is the* first *thing but surely not*
> everything *when it comes to finding a mate. Yes, this is*
> *a pop quiz."*

It is clear to me based on such responses (in addition to what I hear in popular media) that women are utterly and intensely overly preoccupied with the fear of being judged by men (and I'm guessing by other women, too) in terms of physical beauty. Accordingly, women will emphasize character-determining aspects (the opposite extreme of the pendulum) in determining long-term marriage compatibility.

In general, men are hard-wired to respond to elements of physical attraction and women are hard-wired to respond to elements of relational attraction. Both aspects are hard-wired gifts from God. He made our two genders that way. Thus, it's natural for men to seek physical appeal and women for all things relational. But the pendulum swings in each of us; both extremes are a part of us. It may not swing minute-by-minute or even year-by-year; it may also not swing to the same extreme in both directions. Perhaps the direction it swings depends on where God has us in life. For me, being single, being well steeped in sex hormones, my pendulum swings seemingly stuck in the direction of physical attraction. Yes, my challenge during this present swing of my pendulum will be to choose a mate who I will also delight in when the pendulum swings to the opposite extreme (relational attraction).

If you are currently going online to meet Mr. Musing you will most likely be sifting through men seemingly stuck on the physical swing of the pendulum. Well, you can e-mail him an unprovoked essay about how subhuman he is for his current location on the pendulum, or you can look beyond it and into his character. Oh, no. He will not initially be looking beyond your physicality but rest assured, he eventually will. Your role in the meantime is to review your diet and exercise program and your artful use of makeup.

Are you resistant to the idea of attending to your physical beauty in order to attract a mate? Do you take your resistance a step further and actually berate a man for his God-given desire to find a physically appealing mate? Doing so would guarantee you that he will move on immediately. And if you flirt with the notion that you will change a man's focus by resisting his natural desire for a "beauty," you're wasting your time. Why not, instead, spend that time beautifying yourself (i.e., diet, exercise, makeup)? Would that go beyond your pride?

Are you too stubborn or lazy to do that? One last way you can beautify is to admit to him that you understand his desire for a "beauty." Tell him you see God's beautiful plan in using physical attraction in drawing a man in the direction of his mate. Tell him that you desire to be the beauty that God intends you to be (for Mr. Right), even if the man with whom you are communicating claims that you are not his beauty. Who knows? By your not making him feeling subhuman for following his attract-o-meter, he might just find that very attractive in you.

CHAPTER 9

MISS-BEHAVIOR

BUT . . . BUT . . . BUT . . . BUT . . .

I have discussed various parts of this book with single Christian women for feedback. My advice to women to drop hints usually evokes an almost unanimous reply. This reply was discussed in Chapter 6: WOMEN'S REBUTTAL and is repeated here for emphasis. "It's the man's role to step up and be brave enough to face possible rejection and ask a woman out on a date. If he is asking out a woman for godly reasons he should have the godly confidence to do it in the face of possible rejection. It's not a woman's role to drop hints; that's akin to making the first move and that's a man's role."

When I press for more feedback I usually get the following from women: "I want to feel like I'm being pursued; it's an innate need. I want to feel like I'm worth it."

Just recently one woman said, "When a woman doesn't want a man to pursue her she makes clear negative hints so as to repel him. As such when a man senses neutral hints (neither attractive nor repelling), he should take it as if he has a chance with her if he steps up and tries."

That made sense to me. After all, I've seen my share of negative body language. However, after I slept on it I changed my mind. First of all, a woman displaying negative body language to an approaching male assumes that he is a would-be suitor. He may just be interested in talking, like adult human beings will tend to do. How dare anyone assume to know his intentions? I admit that 99.9 percent of the time he is probably feeling her out, trying to learn of the chances that she'll say yes to a date invitation. But I insist that it's *still* not anyone's place to assume it so. Besides, nowhere in the Bible does it say that to love your neighbor is to ward him off with negative hints.

Using negative hints to ward off an unwanted suitor is the mentality of a junior high student. In the adult Christian world we are expected to communicate in a transparent and honest fashion. Moreover, no one should pass up a chance to network with even Mr./Miss Wrong; as genetically unlikely as it might be he/she might have a brother/sister for whom you might feel some chemistry. In Chapter 11 I address the emotional awkwardness of being a party to an unwanted date invitation. I introduce what I consider to be acceptable mature adult responses.

WHAT DOES THE BIBLE SAY ABOUT BEING ASKED OUT ON A DATE?

Nothing! As far as I understand the culture two thousand years ago, there was no such thing as dating. Marriages were arranged by the parents. For their daughter's marriage the parents got together with the parents of a man whom they thought would suit their daughter well and worked out a dowry deal. As such there is nothing explicitly written that governs pre-dating behavior. By pre-dating behavior I refer to the interaction between a man and a woman prior to and after a man asks her out for coffee, a walk in the park, a movie, etc.

Furthermore, when a woman is not interested in a man whatsoever, what are biblically acceptable ways for her to just say no? This book will address that question.

Suffice it to say that without Biblical guidelines, women are left on their own to deal with both Mr. Right and Mr. Wrong. Be assured, moreover, that the way you handle them will have consequences. Depending on how a woman rejects Mr. Wrong will either make him her enemy or make him her advocate among the men whom she *does* want to date. This book advises women on how they can attract attention from her Mr. Right and describes how she can both reject Mr. Wrong and recruit him in her cause for finding Mr. Right.

HURTFUL LIES WOMEN TELL MEN TO IRONICALLY AVOID BEING HURTFUL

The explanation is much simpler than the title of this section. While men are impacted emotionally by a woman's rejection of a date offer, we realize that you are not the end-all in our world (there are other fish in the ocean). Rejection stings for a minute or two, then life goes on. However, when a woman appears to lie about her reason for saying no in order to so-called "avoid hurting his feelings," there is a greater, much longer-lasting pain that takes root in a man. By saying anything *but*, "Oh that's so sweet, but no thank you, Tom," you inadvertently paint an unfavorable picture of not only women but especially Christian women in Tom's eyes. Is it being unfairly unrealistic to expect honesty from women in these situations?

Once your rejection is delivered don't linger on it; divert his attention toward something else. Anything else! Just don't turn your back and walk away. Before you attend a Christian singles group prepare three diversionary topics of conversation. After rejecting a guy you'll be ready with one. Here are a few suggestions. If Tom's date invitation was to a specific event or activity ask him, "How long have you been into Harry Conic Junior music?" Or "Where do you play paintball around here?" "Do you travel far to get to this meeting?" "Have you ever volunteered at the main church for anything?" "Did you grow up around here or are you a transplant?"

The point is that men really do understand rejection by women based on pure chemistry. Besides, that's probably why he asked you out in the first place, for your beauty, not your brains or Christian character. By being honest with him with a "no but thank you." and disarming him with a follow up question you win his respect. By lingering in conversation with him he sees that your "no" means "no" but that does not preclude her from getting to know you as her brother in Christ. Oooooo!! That feels good to me just thinking about it!

F: Select a random man in your singles group. It's good if he is spiritually mature with a sense of humor. Your brother or your father will do just as well. Tell him you need to practice encouraging men in their role of approaching women for dates. Tell him, "I'm not very good at telling a guy "no" when I feel that spending time with him on a date will feel awkward. But I want to reject him honorably, if that's possible." If Mr. Random agrees, then continue. "Here is my premeditated reply. Oh, that's so sweet, Tom, but no thank you." Insert your diversionary question here. Deliver the words with eye contact and a reassuring smile on your face. Placing your open hand on his shoulder or arm momentarily is a great touch, too. Then ask, "How was that? I really do appreciate your feedback."

WOMEN LIE, GUYS PROJECT, WE ARE BOTH TWO-FACED

In other words, we guys will unfairly project one bad experience with a disingenuous woman onto all women, even the good ones. Yes, we men can get some therapy for dealing with our rejection issues, but the likelihood is that we will not. What we do instead is approach women knowing in our minds that they will be lying and doing or saying just about anything to reject us without ever nicely saying, "*No*, but *Thank you*. I'm very flattered by your invitation."

Yet despite what our past experience is saying to us (as we psych ourselves up to ask yet another woman out), the cordial smile on our faces and delightful manner of our efforts at conversation with you will be the evidence of our interest in you. So, yes, men are two-faced when it comes to approaching a woman: internally to us you are liars; externally we put on the Mr. Smiley face just in case we are now approaching the exceptional woman who isn't a liar. That is the living hell inside of us that we men deal with when we walk up to you. We deal with those thoughts in order to meet you with hopes of asking you out.

F: Can you tell when a man is talking to you whether or not he is building up to asking you out? What are his body language cues?

M: Do you remember the very first time you asked out a girl/woman? Did the possibility of rejection ever enter your mind? If you were rejected (and most of us men eventually get rejected), were you ever able to ask out another woman without the lurking fear that she, too, would reject you? How did detecting her hints make it easier for you to ask her out?

WOMEN KEEPING OTHER WOMEN ACCOUNTABLE

What can women do to minimize men's fear of rejection? Well, actually women can't do anything about that, but they can help men get over that hurdle. In addition to his rejection memories as spelled out above he is also reminded of the consequences of asking out women who rejected his invitation.

I call these consequences the "fallout." The fallout is those conversations that go on among women after one of them has been asked out by Mr. Wrong. You know, the hush-hush catty comments about his ineptitude, followed by a synchronized group look across the room at Mr. Wrong with simultaneous snickering. Fear of rejection is natural, but fear of the fallout is a learned fear based on women behaving badly, very badly.

You can't do much about men's fear of rejection; but you can reduce, if not eliminate, the humiliation of the fallout. What you can do is keep your women friends accountable for how they communicate with men during his invitation and afterwards with her friends. For example, let's say Tom just asked out Tiffany. Sure enough within moments Tiffany and her friend Mary are now swapping stories about Tom. Tiffany is understandably emotional about Tom's invitation, and if she doesn't express her feelings to someone she's going to burst.

After explaining to Mary that Tom just asked her out, Tiffany proceeds with derisive laughing at Tom's desirability. Tiffany boasts to Mary about successfully evading Tom's invitation by lying that she would be going out of town the weekend of the date. Mary knows Tiffany lied to Tom in order to curtail his apparent interest in asking Tiffany out. No matter how goofy or undesirable Tom might be to both Tiffany and Mary, Mary would be doing all women (and men, too) a great service by telling Tiffany, "You know Tiffany, I know Tom is no great catch, but you didn't have to lie to him. You could have given him some dignity by being honest with him. Most men can be gallant when they feel a woman is being truthful even if it's in rejection. Why do you feel you have to lie? As Christian women aren't we supposed to be honest?"

Okay, okay, okay. That is a pretty funny quote for Mary to say to Tiffany and a reflection of my own wishful thinking of how I think women should keep each other accountable in such tempting occasions to gossip. Can you imagine keeping your girlfriends accountable by saying that? I know; it's just not going to happen. It's totally laughable! In fact I was mentally laughing the whole way through writing it.

But it's a sad commentary on our church society that such words of accountability should be laughable. In that wishful statement Mary *did* hold Tiffany accountable. Mary *did* live out biblical standards in what she said in response to Tiffany's undignified reactions toward Tom's invitation.

F: Have you ever gotten a good laugh by telling your female friends about the goofy guy who just asked you out? Have you ever been told such a story?

M: You just asked out Tiffany. Do you now sense that you are the butt of undignified comments by the women in her trusted circle of friends?

GREAT ESCAPE STORIES

But why was I laughing as I typed out the wishful reply of accountability by Mary? Is saying that reply to Tiffany unfair or anti-Christian? *No way*! *Not a bit*! Totally to the contrary. Mary's reply is precisely what Mary *should* say to Tiffany in that situation. But given my experience with women my reality is that it's never going to be said from one woman to the next. Women enjoy all too much the bonding in swapping stories of how they narrowly escaped being asked out by Mr. Awkward, I guess much like men like swapping escape strategies of narrowly getting away from the street bulls in Spain.

And the goofier the guy the better the laugh women get out of the escape story, no matter what tactics they use. Moreover, I wonder if the average Christian woman has the moral stamina or backbone to confront other women on such issues. Imagine what doing so would do to Tiffany's relationship with Mary. Tiffany would go off and talk to Sue about what Mary just said to her. Sue would be appalled by Mary's accountability comments to Tiffany, and Sue and Tiffany would walk off together into the sunset as new "best" friends. Isn't that sweet?

But what about Tom? What about Mary? Both are now suffering from unjust treatment from a woman.

F: After rejecting a man have you ever just hung around for an extra minute or two to continue conversation with him? How did you feel during this "follow-up" conversation? How did he seem to feel?

M: Do you feel like continuing your conversation with a woman after being rejected by her? Would this "follow-up" conversation be as unlikely as remaining friends with an ex-girlfriend after a bitter break up?

ONLY 5 PERCENT OF ALL WOMEN LIE TO MEN

You probably agree with me. Mary did in fact say the right thing to Tiffany. You also make it a practice to say such accountability statements to your women friends when it's called for. God bless you. Let's speculate that 95 percent of women would say what Mary said (and also apply that in their own behavior toward men). That's a pretty high percentage. But 100 percent of men are convinced that they have been unlucky enough to only meet the other 5 percent of women who lie. Even if only 5 percent of the women are doing the lying, it is vital that the other 95 percent of the women correct that vicious 5 percent for the benefit of 95 percent of all women (and indirectly 100 percent of men).

Indeed, it is unfortunate that 100 percent of the men would draw conclusions about 100 percent of women based on the behavior of only 5 percent of the female population. There's a word that summarizes our drastic and skewed conclusions: *Stereotype.* Yes, stereotyping is unfair in many ways, but in many other ways it is natural and even vital to our individual survival or at least for drawing general conclusions of our immediate surroundings. For example, you would not walk into a dark alley in a dilapidated section of town where you see three men in dark clothes exchanging something in a plastic baggie. Most of us would not take advantage of this moment as an opportune time to spread the Gospel.

But the small percentage of those who do God's will in this scary example might just learn that two of the men in the alley have momentarily stepped out the back door of the restaurant where they work as deep-fat fryer cooks in a take-out kitchen. The other man has just offered them a sample of fresh cilantro harvested from his uncle's field just outside the city.

Most people will favor safety versus testing their stereotypes. The same goes for men in dealing with women. However, occasionally when a man is inspired by a woman's beauty he *will* test his stereotypes of women by approaching her to converse with the ultimate goal of sensing whether or not she is interested in him. Such a man is the exception in safe Christian singles groups. I will write more about him, Master Brave, in Chapter 14: MISTER BRAVE DOESN'T EXIST, BUT MASTER BRAVE DID . . . ONCE

F: Many frustrated women would end a grocery list of scathing charges against a former boyfriend with the word, "*Men*!" When you hear the word *men* used to convey such hostile feelings what stereotypes are conjured in your mind about men? To what percentage of the male population do you suppose those stereotypes apply?

M: What fears other than fear of rejections do you face when embarking on asking a woman out for a date? What unchristian thing have you personally done to a woman that would confirm most women's general stereotypes about men?

WHAT'S THE POINT OF THE STEREOTYPE EXAMPLE?

I need to be convincing that men's stereotypes of women can impact men's interactions with them. No, most men will probably not ignore women. Most men find women too irresistible to just walk away. But what men will do is bring their stereotypes, hurts, and frustrations of dealing with dishonest women into the first few moments of meeting you. How much fun can his rejection baggage be for you? He is supposed to be fulfilling your expectation of a brave, confident, irresistible, and handsome prince as he asks you out. Instead you get his baggage-modified behavior. I wouldn't blame you for requesting a refund on the male species of the human race.

"Dear God, Eve might have been pretty happy with Adam, but in AD 2000 you might consider releasing a new model of men. Till then I'll take a rain check and keep this voucher. Thank you."

In conclusion you are doing yourself, other women (because another women will eventually marry a guy who has been lied to by a woman), and men a huge favor by being honest with men. It has the effect of restoring in men the blissful naivety they once possessed as boys as they made their first approach to that cute girl in his kindergarten class. Moreover, it is essential to also correct your girlfriend's mean-spirited behavior when she conveys a dishonest great escape story about how she narrowly escaped Mr. Totally Goofy.

F: If/When Mr. Totally Goofy asked you out, what stereotypes of goofiness lead you to conclude that he could never be Mr. Right for you? (i.e., he can never be romantic or suave, never be a leader or someone to be taken seriously, a poor role model to your future children, the last employee to be promoted . . .) Where did you learn that goofy behavior is contrary to romance, good leadership, role modeling, success in career, contrary to loving you as a man should and as a woman desires?

F: Comment on the following statements. Men tend to
      desire a stereotypical, physically beautiful woman.
      That's just the way men are wired. Women on the
      other hand tend to desire a man who is respected by
      other men (i.e. a man's man) and desired by her
      women peers.

AVOIDANCE OR ANTI-HINT STRATEGIES: LATCHERS AND SNATCHERS

I don't know if women do the following out of nervousness, rudeness or fear. Earnest Ernie walks up to two women
as they are chatting at their Christian singles group. He is less
than desirable. Earnest Ernie politely introduces himself and
does his best to smooth out the awkward silent moments with
icebreaker type questions. Just superficial pleasantries really.
    So that lasts about ten seconds before the two women
revert back to their original conversation with each other.
Sensing no chemistry for Earnest Ernie the two women *latch*
their eye contact onto each other at the exclusion of Earnest
Ernie. *Oh*, but yes, Earnest Ernie is still standing in the conversation triangle, but the women exclude him completely
from their attention.
    Earnest Ernie tries his best to pleasantly follow along but
is secretly suffering inside from the gender specific topics they
continue to discuss and the rapid pace with which those subjects change. I don't know how he does it, but Earnest Ernie is
able to interject a relevant comment or introduce a different
and more gender-neutral topic of conversation. The two
women barely notice him but quickly *snatch* his topic and
continue to discuss it while they *latch* on to each other again
at the exclusion of Earnest Ernie. Their body language suggests that the two women would prefer that he go away. Any
outside observer would conclude that in this triangle Earnest
Ernie is being unwillingly tolerated as a source of conversation
fodder but is excluded from the friendship or relationship
building that it fosters between the two women.

Earnest Ernie eventually takes a couple of small steps backward and turns from the two women unnoticed as they continue discussing his topics while they remain latched onto each other. Shortly thereafter a woman walks up to the two women, and they receive her with a big hug. Now there are three women latching on to each other, each one receiving equal inclusion from the other two. Clearly they received her quite differently from the way they received Earnest Ernie.

F: Did Earnest Ernie rudely interrupt the two women's conversation to introduce himself? Should he have waited for them to first separate?

M: If you waited for women to separate from all-women conversation circles would you ever have a chance to speak to one of them?

The Untouchables

The Untouchables of your Christian singles group are the top 5 percent of the men and women in terms of physical attractiveness. Everyone watches them with hopes of getting their attention and dating them. The women in this category don't need to drop hints because the bravest of the brave men will approach them cold-turkey, no subtle hint required. That's the type of attention that these women are used to receiving.

You know who they are. At Christian singles group social events these women bunch up and dance in their own exclusive circle, grandstanding or putting on a show for all the onlookers. For a good laugh, now imagine socially awkward Annie at two hundred and fifty pounds trying to break into their dancing circle bustin' moves like Frankenstein. But the laugh is not on Annie; it's on the Untouchables! Can you see the Untouchables shamefully migrating their circle slowly away from awkward Annie? Such exclusive behavior cuts against the grain of decent Christian behavior.

Due to the Untouchable image that the top 5 percent of women want to portray and preserve, they end up home alone on Friday and Saturday nights. Like all the other women in their Christian singles group the Untouchables will have to realize that most Christian men will not pursue them without a hint from them. Incidentally, I find it most appealing when an Untouchable woman interacts equally with any woman despite social standing. In fact a woman "condescending" to the socially awkward is a personality trait that appeals to me in a woman. If an Untouchable woman will talk to awkward women then she might talk to me too.

Is There An Extra Seat In Your Car?

This next anecdote didn't happen to me, but I was there to witness it as the whole thing unfolded.

A large group of us were standing in the church parking lot, making final carpool arrangements. We were about to head off for a weekend retreat about a two-hour drive away.

One woman arrived just as we were about to finalize things. She was not only an Untouchable but also a high maintenance one at that. She had two big duffel bags plus what appeared to be a suitcase to hold all her vanities. The other women had the equivalent of one duffel bag and a lunch box-size travel bag for vanities.

The Christian singles group leader was positioned in the middle of all the people and parked cars and was about to call everyone's attention to pray for travel safety. There was an expectation of that prayer time and everyone was beginning to hush and focus attention on the leader without being asked

117

to do so. At that moment Miss Untouchable, Tiffany, walks into the center of attention, lugging her bags and making a general announcement. "Does anyone have an extra seat in their car?"

One social awkward, let's call him George, responded, "Yes, I have an extra spot."

I could see a grin and blush coursing across his face with the anticipation of having such a beautiful woman ride in his car for the next two hours. Tiffany was clearly out of his league; she is a 9 while he is 5.

To continue, all eyes were on Tiffany and George. I think I even sensed a hush come over the crowd as we were all amazed that she would even consider being in the same car with an awkward. To his offer she says, "Oh, great! I have a ride in another car, but would you mind taking my luggage?"

I distinctly remember my reaction to her rudeness. I felt my stomach physically cringe and internally I said very loudly, "Oh, God! Why? He's such a nice guy?" It was clearly a case of unintended public humiliation. I am still unable to fathom how anyone, Christian or not, could act in such a shameful manner. She never even once broke her stride. She plopped her bags in the backseat of his car—he already had two people in his car beside himself—made her way to the Untouchable's car, and they were on their way before the departing prayer could be said.

I would like to embellish the story by saying that George was standing by the muffler of the Untouchable's car as it sped off leaving him coughing in a cloud of exhaust. But it didn't happen that way. Nevertheless George maintained his usual easygoing demeanor as we all bowed our heads in prayer for travel safety. No doubt he was suffering inside asking himself, "What just happened here?"

To this day some ten years later George can be found mumbling off in the corner of the singles group meeting room, "Yeah, sure I have an extra spot, yeah, extra spot...room for you...my car...." (Just kidding. He doesn't mumble. He's happily married now, uhm, not to Tiffany.)

DISRUPTING THE NATURAL ORDER OF ATTRACTION

Women are infamous among men for their manipulations of the natural order of attraction. But first let me present a typical complication expressed in a song by the J. Geils band:

"You love her
but she loves him
and he loves somebody else
You just can't win"
(Wolf, Peter and Seth Justman. "Love Stinks". *Love Stinks.* EMI Records, 1980)

Before reading further, grab a pencil and blank paper. Draw out a triangle and write one name at each point including Jane, Marry and Jim. It's a dreaded love-triangle.

Jane and Mary are becoming friends through their Christian singles group. Jane likes Jim and told Mary about her affections for him. However, Mary has always liked Jim, but never told Jane. Jim likes Mary but not Jane. Jim finally musters the courage to invite Mary for coffee. But Mary, thinking it's best to preserve her growing friendship with Jane, rejects Jim's offer. Mary foolishly thinks, "Maybe if I reject Jim, he will ask out Jane. If so, my sacrifice of Jim on behalf of Jane should cement my friendship with Jane." Consequently Jim doesn't have coffee with Mary and will never even consider inviting Jane for coffee because he just doesn't feel attraction for her. In conclusion, because of Mary's immature sense of allegiance to Jane, there are three people now who will be sitting home alone on Friday and Saturday nights.

Mary's rejection of Jim for the "greater" gain of Jane's friendship is a deplorable demonstration of having a false allegiance between two women. In a sense Mary decided to bow out of the "competition" for Jim's affection. Mary really messed up the natural order of attraction between Jim and herself. She, in essence, blew it. The take-home message is that it is unwise to redirect the natural order of a man's God-given attraction for a particular woman.

Curiously what got Mary into this position of having to sacrifice Jim to Jane was the fact that long ago Mary held back on giving Jim hints of her interest in him. By now Mary and Jim would be dating if not engaged. What if, however, both Mary and Jane meet Jim simultaneously and both take a liking to him? Both should drop their hints and let Jim choose. This is the natural course of things. If Jane gets upset with Mary when Jim chooses Mary, then Mary ought to say to Jane, "Grow up, get a life, get a reality check and move on, sister. Maybe Jim here has a handsome friend with whom we can set you up."

FACILITATING THE NATURAL ORDER OF ATTRACTION

Let me end this chapter with some affirmation of my sisters in Christ. My faith in womanhood was actually greatly restored by a sequence of events that occurred to me at a singles picnic.

Through my online matching service, I met Jane. She was interesting to talk to and time really flew by while we sipped coffee. However, the physical chemistry wasn't there for me. But I took the advice of the matching service and met her again to see if something wouldn't spark. Well, after a second meeting nothing sparked. The next day or so I communicated to her pretty much what I just wrote.

I'm sure she was probably a little hurt and/or offended by my frankness. But in practicing what I preach in this book on the topic of rejecting the opposite sex, I wanted to be honest and forthright. In reality, I wasn't sure how she processed my manner of rejecting her, but I could rest assured that honesty is the best policy even if it stings temporarily.

About three months later I attended a local church's singles athletics picnic. I was last in a food line of about two hundred single men and women. I filled my plate and headed for the populated picnic table area. Consistent with my eleven years of experience with Christian singles group, there was a clear separation of men from the women. The main grassy aisle down the center separated groups of women on the left and men on the right side.

Being new to the group I immediately said to myself, "Oh my God! This separation tendency must have followed me from Philadelphia."

I can still see it clearly in my memory walking toward the grassy aisle and saying repeatedly over and over again in my head, "Don't sit with the men. Don't sit with the men. Don't sit with the men. Don't sit with the men." So I walked halfway down the grassy aisle and plopped my plate down on a picnic table asking, "Is anyone sitting here?" The five women at the table said, "No. Please have a seat."

Making that grassy aisle walk was a moment to remember. Looking back on it, I dramatize it in my memory, and it always gives me a good chuckle. Here I go walking down that grassy isle with a plate of food in my hands. Being the last one, many of the people already seated have their eyes fixed on me. As I make it halfway down the grassy aisle heads begin to turn to see where I will sit.

The men are wondering, "Where's he going to sit? Is he going to sit with us for some male bonding or is he going to cross the great divide and sit with the women?"

Now as I make my final steps, I break to slow motion speed for dramatic effect. As my footsteps start heading for the women's table the tables of men start pointing their buddy's attention in my direction. Expressions of tortured mental suspense courses across their faces as if to ask, "Is he really going to do it?"

Now only two steps away from the women's table, one man gags on his iced tea while another chokes on his burger. Many more men let food drop from their mouths as their jaws drop with awe at what they are about to witness. And after I set my plate down and get permission to join the women, the men jump up with loud cheers, tables rocking, plates overturning, and drinks spilling at the eruption of ecstatic dancing, high-fives and high belly bounces. One guy does the moonwalk shouting, "He did it! He did it!!". Then the men, as if instructed by a higher being, immediately outstretch their arms in my direction and bow down exclaiming, "We are not worthy! We are not worthy! We are not worthy oh great one who crossed the great divide."

Okay. Enough dramatics. Do you get the picture? Men are petrified of approaching women, especially when the women are in groups. In doing so I crossed the great divide between single men and single women. Does this example help you realize the practicality of dropping hints?

Now let me get back to the point of this section. I sat down at the picnic table and almost immediately I was introduced to every woman at the table and was the center of attention for about a minute. After the introductions one woman said, "Okay, you just sat in the hot seat, and we're going to ask you some questions about men."

I knew I had crossed the great divide of the grassy aisle, but I didn't realize that I crossed the Continental Divide. For about thirty minutes we discussed all kind of single gender role issues and questions about the opposite sex that we've always wanted to pose but were afraid to ask.

The first thing they said in perfect unanimity was that I was very brave and confident for asking to sit at their table. We then moved to a blanket on the grass overlooking the courts where others in the big group were playing volleyball. We talked another hour there, adding a few people now and again for a broader perspective. It was an unprecedented meeting of minds between the sexes, and it was wonderful.

To my shame I walked away from that event without asking one single woman for her phone number or email address. I can be such a coward. But I haven't yet gotten to my point. In the previous section I talked about how shameful it is for women to disrupt the natural order of a man's attraction, the love triangle and false allegiance of Mary to Jane.

The next day I got a call from Jane (not the Jane from the love triangle example but the two-date Jane for whom I felt no chemistry and told her so).

"Hi, Ed? This is Jane. Remember me from the online matching service?"

"Oh, yeah, uh…. Hi. How are you doing?" *Man! What does she want? I thought I was pretty forthright about my lack of chemistry for her.*

"Oh quite fine. Say I just wanted to let you know that you met some friends of mine at the athletic picnic yesterday. I wasn't able to make it. Do you remember meeting Sue, Kim, and Karen?"

"Oh my gosh, YES! How did you figure out that they were talking about me?"

"Oh, it wasn't that hard—your name, your Ph.D., your general features. Anywhoo, one of them, Karen, is interested in getting in e-mail contact with you, and I was wondering if it's okay to give her your address."

At that moment I was stunned, ecstatic, and disappointed, all in one. I was stunned that a woman I thought might be bitter toward me is now matching me up with her friend. I was ecstatic that the women I talked to on the blanket the day before were very attractive. I was disappointed because I was more attracted to the other woman, Kim.

"Oh, uhh....ummm yea....that ....would be ....great. Okay Jane, I have to tell you what I'm feeling right now. I know this might sound really ungrateful, but I'm feeling it so I have to say it. Um... Karen is an attractive woman, but I was actually more attracted to Kim. Do you think Kim would be interested in e-mailing me?

"Well, I think she would, so why don't I give you both their e-mail addresses and you can meet both of them. I appreciate you asking that. I mean, after all, if you are more interested in Kim, why not pursue her?"

"Yeah, okay, I mean I was just trying to be honest and spontaneous with you. I actually would be honored to have coffee with both of them separately just to learn more about them and what they like to do."

"So here are their e-mail addresses. Yeah, why not meet both of them? I'll let them know that you are interested in both of them, but more so in Kim. I hope you make a connection."

That was the essence of the phone conversation with Jane. I hung up the phone thinking, "Wow! Now there are some brave women playing their role in finding Mr. Right." My faith in women was rekindled at that moment. Within a week or two I met with Karen, the woman who first expressed an interest in meeting me. It was a bit awkward meeting with her since our prior e-mails discussed the issue of me being more attracted to Kim. Having nothing to lose and fellowship to gain, we met. We sat on a park bench in the city and talked for about an hour. We talked about feeling awkward given the circumstances of our meeting and got to know each other a bit.

After meeting with Karen, I met with Kim a few weeks later. It was at a July 4th picnic that she hosted at her town-house. I went there with my flat mate, Anechie. Anechie is from Africa and hadn't yet experienced that holiday with fireworks. I talked to Anechie about the circumstances surrounding meeting Kim, so she knew there might be some further developments between Kim and me at this celebration.

Anechie left that night with a very good feeling about Kim and from that day reminded me of how suitable she was for me. The long and short of it is that I ended up not dating Karen or Kim. I didn't pursue either of them, not due to anything that they could control but because of my dreaded criteria list. When I informed Anechie about writing this book she lectured me about how if I weren't so foolish I would probably be engaged to Kim by now. Despite or in spite of what Anechie said, this book is written and I am still single.

So what's the take-home message of this section? If, after giving Mr. Coffee a chance for a short date, you don't feel chemistry, then if he asks for another date, be honest with your feelings. You are obligated to honesty because first and foremost you are a Christian woman and called to be honest. Second, you need him on your side, your advocate, for finding Mr. Right. He might have an attractive brother or friend that he can introduce to you. Finally, be proactive in your hint dropping behavior; recruit your friends on your behalf if necessary.

M/F: A member of the opposite sex just asked you out. You are not interested in the least. How do you say no? Say it out loud, yes, out loud to yourself as you hold this book. Did you just make an advocate or an enemy in that brave person? Now I know you didn't say it out loud so pick up a pencil and paper and write it out. Then you'll be ready to say it out loud when the time comes. You'll make an advocate, I hope.

CHAPTER 10

PROFILING CHRISTIAN SINGLES GROUPS

WHO GOES TO CHRISTIAN SINGLES GROUPS?

Let me make two broad and bold sweeping generalizations about the folks in attendance of Christian singles group. The women have a history of seducing men for relational benefits and the men have a history of using women for sexual benefits. Okay, so maybe you are not included but remember what Christ said about sexual sins: even the ones in your imagination occur in your heart and therefore count as sin. Are you included now?

In addition to a past history of sexual sin a good percentage of your Christian singles group may still be in its grip. Not one of us is sinless, so that statement should come as no surprise to you. Indeed, all of us probably believe that seducing and using is an offense against God; those sins need to be confessed and repented of and a path of sanctification embarked upon. Consequently in your singles group the women refrain from seducing and the men refrain from using—or at least they both try. In fact both genders in the Christian singles group probably try to be celibate to maintain a good reputation within their Christian singles group. With that said, what kind of atmosphere do we former seducers and users generate in our Christian singles group?

Sterility! Ugh!

Let me explain. Women refrain from dropping hints of interest for fear of reverting back to their seducing ways, and the men no longer pursue for fear of backsliding into their using ways. Is the atmosphere of your Christian singles group lacking in vitality and stifled? Are any of the women engaging in dropping hints? Are any of the men following up and asking them out on delightful dates? If not, this is a disgraceful state of God's single child because the women should be engaging in hint dropping and the men in hint follow-up. There should be hint dropping and date asking; that is, unless the Lord has given you clear indication that He has plans for you to be single.

What does Paul offer to help us with deciphering God's will for marriage in our lives?

"But if they cannot exercise self-control, they should marry. For it is better to marry than to burn with passion." (1 Corinthians 7:9, *The Holy Bible*. English Standard Version)

Notice that Paul doesn't say anything about going to Christian counseling or single sex accountability groups to try and put out this burning passion. Marriage is his simple solution. Accordingly, burning with sexual passion is *not* a complex spiritual warfare issue. It's God's *very loud hint* that He wants you to enjoy His gift of sex in marriage. And getting into a marriage starts with a woman dropping subtle hints. If words like *burn with passion* and *very loud hint* don't describe your sex drive even remotely, then maybe God's plan for you is to be single and, therefore, celibate. If so, this book may not be for you. Also, maybe a Christian singles group is not for you since you won't be contributing to an atmosphere conducive to hint dropping or date asking.

THE OLE' "I'M DEVELOPING A RELATIONSHIP WITH THE LORD" LINE

"Eddie B., what's wrong with the men in this group? Why aren't they asking anyone out?" Getting back to Sherri's question (posed in Chapter 3: THE MILLION-DOLLAR QUESTION), I responded with the following: "I don't want to ask anyone out right now; I first want to learn what it means to have a relationship with the Lord. Meanwhile it's nice to be in fellowship with people in the same life situation."

That's it! I mean, sure, I wanted marriage and family *eventually*. But at that time I really just wanted to learn about what it meant to have a relationship with the Lord. Besides, if I did date and ended up in a bad break-up, I didn't want to face "Miss X" at the Christian singles group every week. In other words one of us would probably have to stop attending the group, sort of a "divorce" settlement. I didn't want to be the one to have to leave. Moreover, I didn't want to screw up the good feeling of being reputation-less as I walked into the Christian singles group every Sunday morning.

Indeed, I did learn something about a relationship with the Lord. I learned about my pride, my very destructive pride. I learned how I would hide behind my former "nice guy" image to avoid dealing with sin issues. My attitude was "not caught, not guilty." It was not a matter of being obedient to God regarding confession of sin but being on the constant guard of a good reputation. Consequently, the attitude I brought to the singles group was that of phoniness.

I didn't realize it at the time, but as I grew in my relationship with the Lord, I began to crave a more spontaneous, less guarded, more honest demeanor. I wanted an existence in which I could confess my sin issues or at least not fear them slipping out. I first got the craving for the taste of freedom from the chains of sin thanks to the transparency of much stronger brothers in the Lord both in and outside of the singles group. I realized how much my prideful "nice guy" image was keeping me separated from the love of God. After all, the main tenet of God's love is that he sacrificed Jesus' life as penalty for my sins past, present, and future.

Sure it's easy enough to understand intellectually; but it took several years for the Holy Spirit to penetrate my heart, hardened with pride. My transparency began to happen one-on-one or in small group discussions. But it took me twelve years to get to a point where I could confess my deepest sin issues in the context of a men's accountability group. As I look back on where I was in this process I realize how I contributed to the sterility of my first Christian singles group with my "nice guy" attitude and lack of obedience to God in an attitude of confession of sin there.

I believe some women (more commonly than men) genuinely want to first learn about what it means to have a relationship with the Lord. Indeed, despite my own earnest desire to have a relationship with the Lord, I still fell in love with a few of the women I met at the Christian singles group. They weren't interested in me, but I fell in love nevertheless.

It seems that many single adults come into the Christian church battered and bruised. They come out of a series of what started out as very wrong relationships gone even worse. This history is true of me, too. That is why good Christian men (at least men who are afraid of God's wrath) will back away from a woman who is in this emotionally battered condition. We can sense that she needs to sort out a path in the direction of Jesus, not toward us. And the last thing she needs is a man who is going to help her do that. She needs a sister, or two or three, without ulterior motives who can better minister to her soul.

However, Christian women who dishonestly use the ol' "I'm developing a relationship with the Lord" as a rejection tactic should also be afraid of God's wrath. Women who use His name in this false manner not only hide from essential character development but also lead men to disbelieve other emotionally battered women who really do need to first forge a path to the Lord. Looking back on my own words, I also needed to grow up and stop using the same excuse for rejecting women to whom I simply was not attracted.

I just wrote that on one hand I wanted to learn about a Lord-relationship; on the other I would have set that desire as second priority if I met Miss Right. It's kind of telling how putting the Lord second parallels Adam's priority in the Garden of Eden with Eve. Anyway, the point is not to blame women for anything like being a temptation; the point is that I would set developing a Lord-relationship as second priority if Miss Right came along. So if Miss Wrong were to ask me out at that time, I would probably have lied, too, and said, "No but thanks; I really want to spend some time as a single person getting to know the Lord." In other words, "You're not my heaven-sent Miss Right so no thank you."

Let me dispel a notion that might be forming in your mind. Notion: Developing a relationship with the Lord and a member of the opposite sex at the same time is unbiblical and impossible. I don't believe you can find that in the Bible anywhere. We are all sinful and if Christians, we are all on the road of sanctification. In fact two Christians in a relationship can help each other along in their sanctification by providing accountability. There are a number of verses that support "a chord of three is not easily broken."

No, I *can* count; the third person in the chord is God. But let's not be naive; add overactive sex hormones to the relationship and the picture gets complicated quickly. Anyway, the point is that you don't have to wait for a sinless lifestyle before you start a God-glorifying relationship with the love of your life.

To conclude on Sherri's question, both men and women may be wearing blinders that force them to focus on developing a relationship with the Lord. There is no lateral looking around at the opposite sex as a consequence, or at least we overdo a God-focus until Miss/Mr Right arrives on the scene. Our God-focus is the excuse for rejecting unwanted suitors. That phony attitude creates quite a sterile atmosphere at your singles group. Ugh!

F: What are some half-truths that you have offered to reject a man?

F: What were some consequences of honestly rejecting a man?

M: Do you prefer women tell you the truth despite the hurt feelings it might cause you or do you prefer that a women lie with an excuse not to go out with you?

M: Right now on the spot imagine that Miss Wrong just asked you out. What do you say to turn her down? It's not so easy, is it?

THE CAVEAT: TIME FLIES

Developing a relationship with the Lord through the input and accountability of members of your gender is amazing. That's where Christian brotherhood starts. It's an amazing feeling of freedom in Jesus to be with the brothers who experience your transparency. So much so that the feeling of bonding overwhelms the longer-term goal of marriage. Call it male bonding. Even as lousy as I am at male bonding relationships, the Holy Spirit worked a miracle in me to become more transparent. So I kind of enjoyed that newfound fellowship, becoming oblivious to the passing of the years.

After seven years in such fellowship, I found myself suddenly aged-out of the singles group. Oooops! I neglected to form similar fellowship bonds with the women of the group. As such be warned that the years will fly by as you enjoy your Christian singles group.

Forming same-gender fellowship bonds honors God in that transparency and accountability relationships develop. But don't put dating and bonding with the opposite sex on hold. In fact, real life sin issues will tend to surface in dating relationships. How you are transparent with these issues will be a test of what you are learning in your accountability relationships. Thus, your behavior in your dating relationships is a healthy reality check on your growth as a Christian man.

BEEN THERE; DONE THAT…WON'T DO THAT AGAIN

I can pretty much detect with my fear-o-meter when a woman has recently come out of an ungodly relationship. Refractory Rita showed up at the Christian singles group one Sunday morning looking for love, the love of Christ, and will look through any guy who gets in her path. Yes, Refractory Rita has a recent past that will shut down any Christian singles group. What I mean by this statement is that well-meaning men in a good relationship with the Lord will fall like bowling pins in the wake of her rejection-emitting body language. She should be promptly escorted to the mother hen of the Christian singles group who will refer her to the church's "women's issues" ministry.

So what's Refractory Rita's background? In her secular life she dropped lots of strong hints, even outright asked men out on dates. Well, her most recent catch turned out to be a bottom dweller, but she didn't find that out until her heart got broken—again. Now here she is appearing at your Christian singles group for the first time. Refractory Rita now has the deepest of convictions that the next guy she dates, if any, will have to be heaven-sent. His recall of Scripture will have to be faster than a speeding bullet; his testimony more powerful than a locomotive, his spirit of leadership and volunteerism must be able to leap tall buildings with a single bound.

Look! Up in the sky! It's a bird. It's a plane. No! It's *Mr. Righteous*! Okay. I stole that line from the introduction of the old *Superman* TV series. The point is that Refractory Rita has unrealistically high standards for her Mr. Righteous. In fact her new standards are not even biblical! Christ does not call us to be perfect because that is impossible for humans. Christ did not come to heal the healthy. We are however called to confess and repent of our sins and to be constantly engaged in our path of sanctification. Refractory Rita has no tolerance for such imperfection; she wants a squeaky-clean man who's not going to use her and break her heart in the end.

Sadly for Refractory Rita, each and every man at the Christian singles group is sanctification in process. She has lots of maturing to do. She needs to learn that truly living a Christ-centered life means losing everything to be His daughter, even if it compromises the unbiblical squeaky-clean image she has of Mr. Righteous.

Here's the point of this section. Refractory Rita took to kick-starting relationships with Mr. Wrong by pursuing men, maybe even asking them out on dates. They eventually used her and broke her heart. Consequently Refractory Rita concludes that she cannot trust herself when it comes to finding Mr. Righteous. So now she trusts the Lord to bring her Mr. Righteous. This decision is obviously a good one, right? Yes! But Refractory Rita takes it to an extreme such that she will not even so much as look in the direction of the man that she fancies let alone drop him a hint of her interest. After all look what that got her before: a broken heart.

So Refractory Rita will wallow along in life avoiding relationship risks by looking the other way when Mr. Righteous is in her view. It is tragically cemented in her mind that if a man is of God then that man will find his way to her apartment door with no hint of interest from her. It is emotionally easier for her to be single than it is to take responsibility for the outcome of her former self-motivated pursuit behavior. So she hides behind the Lord in an unbiblical way thinking that when God does send a man to her apartment door it will be a "nobrainer" of a sign that God sent him.

Refractory Rita paints a grim picture. Her high expectations of Mr. Righteous will not only keep her single but also put a damper on the fertile atmosphere of any Christian singles group into which she walks. It's difficult enough in a Christian singles group to create an atmosphere in which Cupid's bow and arrow have some potency; letting in women like Refractory Rita is akin to ripping Cupid's bow and arrow out of this cherub's innocent hands and breaking them over your knee.

Refractory Rita has unnecessarily taken an extreme position on pursuing men. She won't do it or anything that resembles it. The remedy, however, to her experience with Mr. Wrong is quite simple. 1) First understand that no man is going to be sinless. Have this expectation at the outset. 2) *Drop subtle hints*. Sorry, but there is no way of leaving the game of attracting the man you like. There is biblical support for your active role in attracting Mr. Righteous. See Ruth 3:1-6, the account of her laying at the foot of the Boaz the man she was advised to attract. 3) Rebuke Satan when he laughs at you and accuses you of forgetting the heartbreak you received the last time you dropped a hint to a man. Satan revels when he derails two Christians coming together in the name of the Lord. Do you remember God's conversation with Satan? "The LORD said to Satan, "From where have you come?" Satan answered the LORD and said, "From going to and fro on the earth, and from walking up and down on it." (Job 1:7, *The Holy Bible.* English Standard Version)

In my Bible in the footnote it says, "Satan means accuser." So you can guess what Satan was doing as he was going back and forth—accusing man of his sinfulness.

Refractory Rita is in an emotional state that is extremely vulnerable to Satan's accusations. In short Satan accuses not only Refractory Rita but also all of us of not being good enough to be a Christian let alone be someone's spouse. When she hides behind God (the old "I'm developing a relationship with the Lord and no one else right now), Satan wins. No, she is not placing healthy trust in God; she is simply using God to ward off godly men.

4) When Mr. Righteous responds to your hints, count it a blessing of the Lord and take responsibility for getting to know him in a biblical way. If you don't trust yourself alone with him, then take responsibility for making your dates group activities or meet somewhere in public. Tell him about your accountability partner, how you will keep her abreast of how your relationship with Mr. Maybe Righteous progresses.

If you don't have accountability partner then *get one and get one fast*! Telling him you have such an accountability partner does two things: 1) If his interest in you is sincere it will force him to behave, because if he doesn't he could get a well-deserved bad reputation, and 2) If he simply intends to use you he will back off and back off fast also for fear of a well-deserved bad reputation.

A DIFFICULT DILEMMA TO RESOLVE

Perhaps new single adult Christians who have been battered by the secular relationship world should not go to Christian singles group. After all, someone battered by the secular world needs to focus on learning what it means to have a relationship with the Lord. In a Christian singles group by contrast most seasoned attendees will be preoccupied with finding a spouse. Don't get me wrong. There will be much emphasis on defining, describing and continued development of personal relationships with the Lord. And seasoned attendees will participate in such personal relationship developments. But they will be well on their journey with the Lord. Indeed, seasoned attendees will be anxious and preoccupied with moving on to a Christ-focused marriage. New attendees however will probably not be ready to trust.

The dilemma is determining how to welcome untrusting new attendees while keeping the atmosphere of the singles group conducive to hinting women and men who step-up.

F: Do you remember when you woke up one morning with the epiphany that you are now ready to be in a God-glorifying relationship with the opposite sex?

F: When you observe a seasoned Christian woman who is ready to be in a God-glorifying relationship and approachable to Mr. Right, does her behavior around men make you cringe? Does she come across to you as "desperate"?

M: Was there ever a time in your journey as a Christian that you stopped looking or hoping for Miss Right in favor of focusing on a Lord-relationship?

M/F: What short pithy statement would you add to your weekly singles group bulletin to establish the dating tone of the group? For example, "At Christian singles group xyz an active dating life is encouraged even expected from marriage-minded attendees."

For The Sake of the Christian Singles Group

This topic is perhaps the most difficult for me to address because it reveals my sin. My sin is one of intolerance of needy people. I'm actually very accepting of needy people in everyday circumstances, but I don't believe their needs will be met in a Christian singles group. I also believe that needy people attending a Christian singles group will lead to its eventual demise. So who are needy people and where do they fit in?

Needy people are those with mental or physical handicaps that keep them from fully participating in Christian singles group activities. More important than this criterion, however, is the question of longevity of the Christian singles group. Are such people going to attract new members to the group or will they repel new members? This question is essential. In order for a Christian singles group to survive, it must define the "clientele" that it targets and redirect others to church resources that address their needs.

It's easy to imagine that once the emotionally unstable, the drug addicted, the chronically homeless, the chronically unemployed, the grossly over- or underweight, the rude and the crude sprout roots in a Christian singles group, they are unlikely to leave by finding a compatible mate. As such they, over time, become a majority in the Christian singles group, and it ultimately heads for critical mass. Anyone who has ever attended a Christian singles group probably knows the quality of people that I categorize as needy. Sure, the needy give the group an interesting atmosphere, but most people in attendance are praying for a mate, not a freak show to watch.

As a Christian singles group, however, each of us Christians in attendance are called to be inclusive of the needy in our walk with the Lord. Yet if our inclusiveness prevents the needy from getting their needs met, are we really helping them by including them? Let's face it; we have a challenge enough with keeping ourselves together without the added challenge of keeping someone else together. There are professionals who help the needy for a living. We should not be expected to do their jobs when we are ourselves are so mentally challenged by this thing we call finding a mate and carving out a career for ourselves as we wait. I recommend that Christian singles group be selective about who they admit at the same time being prepared to redirect excessively needy people to the church resources that address their needs more fully.

WHO BELONGS IN A CHRISTIAN SINGLES GROUP?

The following recommendation to resolve these two groups of Christians (i.e., the new battered or excessively needy Christian and the once-battered but now seasoned Christian) may sound harsh, and indeed it probably is. Nevertheless, I recommend that newly saved Christians of say less than a year be asked not to attend the Christian singles group. Instead they can be directed to small group Bible studies or less structured care groups where their relationship wounds can be confessed and repented of and addressed by members of the same sex. Separating unseasoned Christians from the seasoned ones in the Christian singles group has an important impact. Mainly the atmosphere in the Christian singles group will be conducive to men stepping up to the pursuit plate. The women and men have had a year to resolve their emotional traumas incurred during their formerly unsaved circumstances. In essence attendees should be "ripe" for a relationship—or at least a date for coffee.

More realistically, attendees will have resolved those issues by the help of the Holy Spirit, had a morning epiphany about being okay to pursue a relationship, and are ready to put themselves in behaviors and social situations conducive to dating. This change of focus from strictly a Lord-relationship to a Lord-relationship-significant-other is equally true of the men and women in the group. Indeed, by separating out the newly saved Christians from the Christian singles group an atmosphere akin to a social dance can be created.

My experience with such social dance events comes exclusively from my attendance of big band swing dances. The atmosphere in these dance halls is heavenly. It is heavenly particularly for guys who when they ask a woman to dance it is almost unacceptable for the woman to say no. Moreover, it is the norm to find a different partner after each song is played. By the end of the night you will have met anywhere from five to twenty new people. It's *wonderful*! Well, maybe wonderful for the men because they get to do the choosing. Women on the other hand can be stuck with a guy with two left feet, and she has to deal with it for the next four minutes or so.

The point is that the rejection factor in the dance hall is greatly reduced, and men quite naturally step up to the pursuit plate if only to find a partner for the next dance. By separating out the newly saved Christians, a similar atmosphere can be generated in your Christian singles group. In fact, I would go so far as to suggest that it be proper etiquette for the women of the Christian singles group to accept an invitation for coffee if she is asked. After all, it's just coffee or a walk in the park or a free cultural event at your local university campus. Limit your meeting to fifteen minutes, but don't make other plans following it just in case chemistry strikes. You might actually enjoy his company for thirty minutes or more.

Of course there are newly saved Christians who can contribute to this kind of social atmosphere in the Christian singles group. They should be welcomed into the group. Actually, any newly saved single Christians should be welcomed into the Christian singles group. But there should be some kind of statement of policy that forewarns new members of the active coed mingling of which they are asked to be a part. After all, it is an active singles group, not group therapy or a place to lick previous relationship wounds.

To conclude, if a woman is not willing to accept an invitation to coffee by the first guy who asks—be he Mr. Righteous or otherwise—she probably shouldn't be attending the Christian singles group. If your definition of your Mr. Right includes that he would *never* condescend to attend a singles group then you should seriously get out of the group and instead volunteer for your church. If you are simply looking for same-gender fellowship, check with your church about small groups; you should not be ignoring the opposite sex in your Christian singles group.

More to the point, when new people show up at a Christian singles group everyone in the room knows they are there to find Mr./Miss Righteous because regular attendees are there for the same reason. If newbies put on a phony facade to the contrary everyone else in the room will know it and gauge the newbies' character by it until they snap out of their ruse. In the meantime newbies go about emitting body language that they are righteous since they are "waiting on the Lord" for the provision of Mr./Miss Righteous, no active effort on their own part. They may even actively repress the desire to date depending on the circumstances leading up to their appearance at the singles group (i.e. broken heart, physical/mental abuse by the opposite sex etc..). These symptoms amount to mental unavailability. These symptoms lead to a sterile dating environment in the singles group. If both newbies and regular attendees cannot at least be open to coffee with anyone who asks, then they should not be going to the Christian singles group; they're just spoiling the dating atmosphere.

Another way that Christians derail their own chances of finding Mr./Miss Righteous in their singles group is to give the group a reputation to others outside the group. Some Christian singles groups, either fairly or unfairly, gain the reputation of being a "meat" market. Chances are, if attendees are inclined to put on a phony facade of righteousness they may shun others who do not. Phonies may be harboring feelings of envy or jealousy because others feel free in the name of the Holy Spirit to pursue the opposite sex, a natural and, therefore, a God-created inclination. Phonies may then go outside of the group to complain about it.

In the future when you hear of someone referring to your singles venue as a "meat" market, take a moment to correct him and say, "Yes, it *is* a 'meet' market; I enjoy meeting many brothers and sisters in Christ there. Is there something biblically wrong with that?" That naysayer is likely to respond, "Nothing wrong if they are not tempted beyond what they are able to handle." Then, with the toe of your shoe, drag your foot across the floor in front of him in a straight-line saying, "Let you without sin be the first to walk across this line and cast the first judgment against us."

That should shut him up.

F: Do you know of Christian women who are just average in beauty but somehow manage to attract the attention from a lot of men? How do you think they do it? Have you ever dared to try that yourself? What were the consequences?

M: What qualities in a woman do you find can easily compensate for average superficial beauty?

SEE ME WORK

Let me introduce Miss Prudence. She has wisely completed her college education with the goal of career and financial independence. She's even taking a graduate school course or two every year toward an MBA. She is focused on her career and doing well. Unfortunately her love life suffers. It's suffering because she is focused on career but not dropping hints. As such, the more her love life suffers, the more she focuses on her career, the less hints she drops the more her love life suffers, the more she focuses on her career . . . the vicious circle. Make no mistake; what kicks off the vicious circle is a focus on career and independence at the expense of a healthy dating life. What would absolutely end the vicious circle is not giving up a career focus but to start dropping hints.

If you are sure that your career will reward your life with blessings beyond those of a marriage and family, then I suggest that you stick with it. Not many people will have such a career. Most importantly, is your career what the Lord wants you to pursue? If so then you probably don't belong in a Christian singles group. Body language of dedicated career women will only suck the fertile hint-dropping verve from the room. Perhaps you would be a greater blessing to the Lord by starting some kind of Christian-based business/science/art networking group. But let me state with clarity: A woman with this much devotion to a career can *still* contribute to the dating atmosphere of a singles group; she just has to be willing to drop hints.

Sadly, from my experience, it is unlikely that such career focused women will. In all honesty it is not "of the Lord" that they refuse to drop such hints. Instead it is of their pride, their very, very destructive anti-God, anti-man or pro-independence pride.

Another anti-God state of mind is that of independence from anyone else's help, even God's. Independence states, "I don't need you, God." And as we know this statement is akin to saying, "I don't need anyone but myself."

Before you walk into your Christian singles group ask yourself the following question. Will I contribute or detract from a healthy dating verve when I am among single Christians?

THE RESIDUE OF THE BATH WATER

The women's movement has thrown out the baby (useful traditions for getting matched/introduced in married) with the bathwater (men's oppressive control over women). After tossing that dirty water out the window, the vessel holding all that water is still dirty with male residue. The vessel is tossed to the side without cleaning and the residue becomes baked into the vessel walls. Now it sits in storage as you raise your children without the help of your ex-husband.

Oh, but he comes around every other weekend or so with his younger girlfriend or wife to take the kids for a weekend. If you were born and raised in America, there is a 50 percent chance that a divorced parent raised you. It's very likely that you spent most of the time with your mom. Here's a personal question. Was your mom bitter at all toward your dad? When Dad showed up for visitation, did Mom's mood or attitude change?

What I'm getting at here is that young children are impressionable. They may have sadly picked up on their mom's attitudes toward men. If your mom is bitter, she will show no signs of delight as an available man approaches her with the possibility of romance. She will likely be displaying body language that screams, "BACK OFF, YOU S.O.B.! YOU'RE NOT GOING TO DO ME LIKE MY EX DID." Can you see how these attitudes toward men might rub off on her impressionable children? You might have been indoctrinated by your mom into resisting or avoiding men. Combine such sour nurturing with your own dating experiences with boys or young men and you have pretty much a lethal combination that will "wash that man right out of your hair."

What if your mom was rather neutral toward her ex, your dad? She neither bad-mouthed him nor extolled his virtues in front of you. Mom also felt she could not stomach that mother-daughter talk where mom is supposed to teach her young adult daughter about the beauty of God's creation called man. With the backdrop of a successful loving marriage the mom would be on the verge of tears of joy while not so successfully conveying to her daughter in a confusingly poetic context the utter being of beauty that a woman is to a man. Then Mom proceeds to describe a sort of unstructured dance that occurs between a man and a woman when they first meet. Two people play their parts in the dance of attraction and courtship with all the inherent subtlety of the nuance.

It goes without saying that if you were too young when you had this conversation, you might have ended that talk by concluding, "MOM, WHAT-EVER." Nevertheless, your mom's joyful emotion will stick in your memory probably for the rest of your life. One day, when you've got the burn to be

142

married, you will understand, and the essence of your mom will guide your subtle body language when you're in the presence of Mr. Right.

Honestly I don't know if this conversation ever happens between a mother and daughter. But it helps me make a point. Imagine that your mom never had that conversation with you. Now figure in that your parents divorced at an early age. Now add several teaspoons of bitterness to your mom's attitude toward men. Do you think these conditions will impact your body language around Mr. Right? At worst you may be repelling him with out even intending to. At best you may give him a sense that you don't even notice him. Whatever your family background is, you can easily remedy it by simply dropping hints.

TAKING INVENTORY

Let's pause for a moment and review. What experiences or expectations are likely to influence women's reactions to men's romantic pursuits? Girls experience the "yucky-ness" of boys early on; in their teens, young women experiment with dropping hints (oftentimes not so subtle hints) and experience the hurt and sexual "piggy-ness" of young men. Equal rights, college education, and career leads to independence from men for pursuit of happiness. During college or shortly thereafter a broken heart over Mr. Wrong sends you to the local Christian church. You discover what it means to develop a relationship with the Lord. After a recovery period from Mr. Wrong, you find your way to the Christian singles fellowship meetings. You are quickly invited to a home-based women's Bible study group where you enjoy fellowship, intimacy, and bonding with God through the women. You are spiritually on the right track. You decide to put full effort into your nascent career and whatever energy you have left you devoted to the women of your Bible study.

Enter Mr. Right. Let's be honest; it's going to take one heck of a handsome man to turn your head at this point. Moreover, and statistically speaking you're probably not a supermodel, so Mr. Handsome is not going to pay you much mind anyway. So for you Mr. Average will try his best to get your attention while you, at best, are barely noticing Mr. Handsome. You are not dropping hints to Mr. Handsome, so what chance does Mr. Average have?

Basically *none*. You are spiritually and emotionally unavailable to men. If most of the women in the singles group are likewise unavailable, will the atmosphere in the group be conducive to dating and marriage? Basically *no*. Should you in your unavailable condition be attending a Christian singles group? *Absolutely not*! Perhaps meeting with an older married woman would be the best mentor for a Christian woman at this time in her life.

That summary ends on a pretty grim note (i.e., that women should not be in a Christian singles group at this time in her Christian walk). The good news is, however, that all she needs to do to be warmly welcomed into a Christian singles group is to start dropping hints. Does that suggestion cause a flare-up of your destructive pride saying, "I don't need to drop hints to men; it's their job to step up cold-turkey"? If so please check that attitude at the door or just stay home during your singles group meetings; the men will appreciate it.

STILL A CHILD AT HEART

Can you believe that your childhood experience with the opposite gender will predispose your expectation into adulthood? Yes, as adults it is true that on the physical level there is a new force of attraction that wasn't there in childhood, namely hormones. Yet on the mental realm there is serious mental repulsion due to earlier childhood unpleasantness with the opposite sex. Men and women with lots of childhood unpleasantness are probably going to have a hard time getting together despite the newfound hormone-induced physical attraction. Indeed, a collision between a man and a woman by Brownian motion (Brownian motion is random movement that a molecule naturally exhibits) would probably be more likely to bring two people together.

Yet the force of physical attraction for many adult men and women simply just isn't enough impetus to counter the fear of rejection or hurt instilled by the scars of childhood. A woman's subtle hints are a panacea for everything that ails a man's heart. I don't know what the panacea is for women to get over their childhood scars enough to drop hints. Perhaps figuring that out should be prerequisite for them to join a local Christian singles group.

CHAPTER 11

THE "R" WORD

AN UNBELIEVABLE QUESTION

I participated in a Christian singles weekend retreat where the women outnumbered the men by about three to one. In an open question and answer session with the guest speaker, one woman asked the following question.

"This is a question for the men. What's the preferred way of telling men no, when they ask us out and we're not interested?"

I wonder how many women in the room were silently asking, "You mean *you* are lucky enough to be asked out?"

Based on the low level of feminine appeal that this woman had, I won't share with you what was going on in my head. Suffice it to say that I was very surprised that she was preoccupied with being asked out . . . by anyone. I thought it was a pretty good question, but her physical appearance and attitude made me laugh inside, uncontrollably. I was glad, though, that someone asked that question.

Another man answered her quite succinctly. I won't tell you at this time what he said, but I simply joined him in saying, "*That's it. Period!*" The emphasis here is that I was in full agreement with what the man said. Hence, I felt unexpected affirmation to write on the topic of the "R" word, REJECTION. I'm not talking about men's fear of rejection; I'm talking about women's inability and what appears to be fear of dishing out rejection to an unwanted suitor.

F: How many men have asked you out over the past six months? How many second or third, etc., dates did you go out on with the same guy? What circumstances do you attribute to your answers?

M: How many women have you asked out in the last six months? If you say less than eighteen (three dates per month) don't fret; the women above who have had less than nine dates are reading this book. They will hopefully be ready to drop hints by the end of this book. You can also increase your numbers by recommending this book to the women in your Christian singles group.

WOMEN HAVE THE RIGHT TO REJECT

I want to point out that I don't judge a woman over her reasons for rejecting my offer for coffee. I am, however, admittedly very harsh on those who use any reason that is a lie. In an ideal world where every unmarried person has read this book, men would not bother asking out a non-hinting woman. He knows those guidelines because he read my book. No hint to him equates to no interest in him. We men get it. Yet not all singles will read this book, so the climate in Christian singles group will be that some men will ask you out regardless of whether or not you drop him a hint. In the following sections I'll arm you with some acceptable and esteeming rejection lines.

You are a Christian woman and, as mentioned previously, you have your own preconceptions of what the essence of your future husband (Mr. Musing) will look like. That is natural. But what kind of flexibility do you allow for the workings of the Holy Spirit in your mental image of Mr. Right? No, I'm not going to lecture you on how you should drop your criteria list or that unrealistic template framing your preconceived Mr. Musing. We are all unique and, therefore, have a unique image in our mind and being of who Mr./Miss Musing will be. That mental image is a consequence of a person's memorable experiences in combination with their less tangible subconscious memory. And it is safe to say that because you are still alive that mental image is constantly being updated by new experiences.

Some would argue that in their Christian singles group only a few people are alive, but let's focus on the bigger picture here. A logical conclusion is, therefore, that experiencing coffee with a man who is interested enough in asking you will impact your preconceived template of your Mr. Musing.

Maybe your experience with Mr. Coffee (who is also possibly Mr. Right) will affirm your preconceived template (i.e., "I'm definitely not liking what he just said/did.") or cause that template to bend a little in his direction (i.e., "Oh my! What he just said/did was intriguing. I would like that characteristic in my future husband. I really must update my antiquated template of Mr. Musing.").

So it's a win-win situation for you and Mr. Coffee. He gets a chance to spend some one-on-one time with a woman he's obviously interested in, and you get to test and or update your preconceived template of Mr. Musing. The only loss is perhaps your time. And if your life is so precisely timed and your weekly schedule booked weeks in advance, then I ask you this question: What other man do you have penciled in for a coffee date? What other hobby or interest of yours did you miss because you accepted a date with Mr. Coffee? By the way, three hours of prime time TV watching per night or yakking/texting on the phone does not constitute an interest or hobby.

So what's the point? If you feel no chemistry for Mr. Coffee, put your feelings aside and accept his offer for coffee anyway. At worst you will get to know a brother in Christ.

Besides, if you are sure that Mr. Coffee will always be just Mr. Coffee he will be glad, nevertheless, that you at least gave him a chance if only for one date.

What if you just don't feel interested in *any* of the men in your Christian singles group? My friend offered me a good suggestion after a phone interview I had with a prospective employer. She said, "Don't say anything that would get you cancelled off their list. Be honest about your credentials but don't give them a reason to count you off. First secure a job offer and a job. Once you're at the final stage of being hired, negotiate over the minutia that you're concerned about. But first secure an offer."

In other words, accept dates with Mr. Coffee. Go out for coffee or a walk in the park. If no physical or spiritual attraction forms, move on. What do you have to lose but an hour being outside of your dwelling place? But first and foremost be of the mindset that it's good to secure a date be he Mr. Coffee or Mr. Musing. If at the end of the first date you still don't sense any attraction or intrigue, thank him for his company but do not accept another date. If he presses you for a reason, you should be honest about the lack of chemistry or intrigue and he will be esteemed, not offended. He will mostly be ecstatic that a girl as pretty as you gave a guy as awkward as he a chance in the first place.

There are other ways that you might benefit. It's the end of your first date, and Mr. Coffee asks if you would care for a second date with him. You turn him down in a dignified manner. Mr. Coffee is hurt momentarily but recovers promptly. He likes your style, and you've just made an advocate for yourself. He will likely respect you for your honesty and even help you in your quest for Mr. Right; he might have a good-looking brother or friend to introduce to you. So esteem him.

Moreover, other men will learn that you give a guy a chance and maybe this knowledge will inspire Mr. Right to ask you out for coffee. "Man! If she'll go out for coffee with that socially awkward guy, she'll *definitely* give me a chance."

Finally, if you don't take this approach to dating and you instead reject men in an undignified manner, you will soon earn a reputation of being stuck-up, snobbish, or worse. In that case not even Mr. Half Right will want to be seen with you for fear of gaining a reputation simply by association with you.

F/M: What childhood memories do you have of male/female role models that might contribute to your Mr./Miss Right template in your mind?

Pushy Guys

Admittedly some guys might push women for more details about why they reject them. Here's a line to memorize. "You know, Ed, I'm sorry, but I just don't feel that kind of chemistry for you." That's it. Say no more. That's pretty much what the man said at the singles weekend mentioned above in section An Unbelievable Question (i.e. the woman's question, "What's the preferred way of telling men no, when they ask us out and we're not interested?"). He will understand and respect you for your honesty, because after all it is only chemistry that inspired him to ask you in the first place. It's man-speak. If he still persists for more details he will only respect you if you turn and walk away from him, preferably to a man who you know will send him away if necessary.

I had an interesting experience with a pushy woman. I was twenty-four and had just graduated from college. I was at a friend's apartment party one Friday night. It was a small party and by the time I got there around midnight it was almost over. There were about five people including an obese woman.

I decided to hit the bathroom then leave. The bathroom was down the dark hallway beyond the two bedroom doors. After flushing and putting the seat back down, I walked out of the bathroom and was about halfway down the hall when Obese Oprah who was heading to the bathroom stopped in front of me.

"Will you escort me home? I don't live too far away from here."

Needless to say, I was caught off guard. First of all, I hadn't very often gotten such a request. Second, I not only felt no attraction to her, I was somewhat repulsed by her obviously overweight condition.

"I . . . um . . . I . . . uh . . . uh . . ."

She takes a step closer to me.

"Will you walk me home?"

"I . . . um . . . I . . ." (Now trying to look beyond her into the living room to see if anyone was watching that I could signal for help.)

She takes a step closer, and now I'm forced to take a step backward deeper down the dark hallway.

"Will you take me home? I really want you to take me home."

"Uh,,.erhh...I...uh... don't think I can do that."

Now don't get the idea that at that time in my life I was Mr. Morality when it came to pursuing women, that is, women to whom I was attracted. At that time I admittedly had taken women home at the slightest suggestion that she would accept my invitation. But I never, ever, seduced a woman for whom I felt no attraction. Wait, okay, there was one woman. Shame on me.

"Why won't you take me home? Why?"

She steps forward again and again I step back.

"I... can't.....umm..... uh....well...."

She steps forward again and again I step back now with my back against the end of the hallway wall.

"Why won't you take me home tonight?"

I finally said, "I'm just not attracted to you in that way."

She took a step away from me and replied,

"Thank you."

With that she turned and walked away.

F: Why do you think it is that men want a clear yes or a
no answer from you when they ask you for a date?

HEART-BREAKING STORIES OF WOE

New Christians want to learn more about developing a
relationship with Christ. But some women use Christ as an
escape strategy for rejecting Mr. Awkward. We men might be
Neanderthals, but we're not dumb. We know that despite any
of your professed stories of pain and woe from prior failed
relationships you are driven by your physical senses.

If a guy walks into the room with hair, black as a raven's
and eyes as engaging as doves, a body like Michelangelo's
"David," (Florence, Italy. circa 1503,) and a sense of humor
like your mellow grandfather's, you will melt like ice cream in
his hand. My knowledge of biology helps me know that this
flip-flop on the part of women is true.

Let's assume for a moment that Mr. Fabulous just broke
off an engagement with Sally after seven months. Sally was,
and still is, devastated after being scorned by him. Four
months later she decides that seclusion at home was at one
time necessary but now is unhealthy. So she decides to check
out the local Christian singles social group. Surely the men
there will treat her better. She decides it's time to get back in
the groove of being with people, people unlike Mr. Fabulous.

Yet the last thing on her mind is getting into a relationship
with a guy. She may have been devastated to the point where
she is for the first time hungry for solace in the Lord. Indeed,
failed relationships can take a heavy and lasting emotional toll

on us. But if such scars incapacitate our physical senses—that is, our desire for the opposite sex—I believe our race would have become extinct millions of years ago.

Most people probably have some negatively impacting incident in their lives brought on by the opposite sex. Maybe it was a kindergarten classmate who pulled your hair and made you cry. You were devastated. But then hormones hit, and that memory has probably still not completely gone away; it's who you are. Nevertheless, you proceed to uncontrollably crave the opposite sex. I bet that you still know by name the kindergarten kid who pulled your hair. Furthermore, if pushed to recall all the fine details, you would blush with innocent passion at the memory—with the exception, of course, of the actual pulling of the hair.

My point is that we are ruled by our physical senses, which are, by the way, a blessing from the Lord. God designed us such that while maybe not fully forgetting our hurts we are hopelessly ruled by our physical senses and desire for the company of the opposite sex. The priority that the Lord put on our physical senses assures the survival of the human race in this admittedly cruel, cruel world. So please, if you aren't attracted to Mr. Awkward when he asks you out don't float him a lie about how your heart was recently broken and you're not interested in dating *anyone* for a while.

F: Have you ever used the evasive date-avoiding excuse that you just recently got out of a long relationship? Did you use the line equally with Mr. Wrong as well as Mr. Musing?

M: If ever given the "I just got out of a long relation-
       ship" rejection line, did you   believe her? What
       went through your mind immediately after she said
       these words?

THE PERFECT REJECTION LINE

My first experience with Christian singles group was
through the Catholic Church. I was twenty-five, single, and
after doing things my own way since turning eighteen, I
wanted to take a second look at the Catholic Church local to
where I was raised. No, it wasn't turning over my will to the
Lord; it was just the preliminary phase of investigating the
meaning of Christian spirituality. Anyway, my younger sister
at the age of nineteen years was asking similar spiritual questions at the university's Catholic campus chapel. Both she
and I discovered the nondenominational Protestant church
shortly thereafter. Any way, she invited me to a newly
formed Catholic-sponsored singles group. It was an informal
group with an average attendance of about twenty people.
Regular attendees were invited to pick a topic that interested
them, make a presentation, and lead a discussion. I picked a
topic near and dear to my heart. I addressed the question,
"How do you deal with rejection from the opposite sex?"
    As you can imagine this topic sparked some pretty good
group discussion. The presentation I made was provocative.
My sister agreed to help me dramatize three different ways
that women typically reject Mr. Wrong. At that time I must
have been experiencing a lot of hurt feelings from women as
a consequence of rejection or at least perceived rejection.
Read on.
    The three ways a woman can deliver rejection were dra-
matized as 1) no reply at all (avoid giving an answer); 2) the
hurtful rejection (i.e., lying); and 3) the esteeming rejection.
In short my character, Bob, worked in the same office building with my sister's character, Tiffany. They both knew each

other, but not very well. Bob met up with Tiffany on the out-door park bench during lunch. That's where Bob proceeded to ask out Tiffany. In all three scenarios the actions and dia-logue leading up to Bob's invitation were exactly the same: the way he walked up to her, where she was sitting, what they talked about briefly before Bob's big invitation. Each scenario ended, however, with Tiffany's response (1, 2, and 3 above) to Bob's invitation.

After each scenario we stopped and opened the floor up to discussion over Tiffany's response to Bob's invitation. In response #1 Tiffany's "no reply" left Bob without a yes, no, or even a maybe. Tiffany managed to skirt the question alto-gether, leaving Bob feeling as if he never invited her out and unacknowledged for his gesture.

In response #2 Tiffany replied with excuses like, "I have to wash my hair. I have a lot of laundry to catch up on. I have to walk my cats and wax my back. Etc." I can't remem-ber the exact dialogue, but you get the picture.

In preparation for my night of leading the singles group, my sister and I sat down to write out the dialogue. But when it came to Tiffany's 3) esteeming rejection line, we both drew a mental blank. Looking back on it, such a creative road-block is indicative of our lack of experience of ever having dealt with rejection in an esteeming manner. For the life of us we couldn't come up with anything. So we decided that on the night of our skit we would go through the drama of sequence #3 and end it just before Tiffany responds with her compassionate rejection line. At that moment we turned to the audience and asked, "Okay, what do you think an esteeming rejection line would be for Tiffany to say right now?"

I honestly don't remember the suggestions or discussion that followed except I do remember the feeling of awkward-ness in the room. We *all* struggled with coining the phrase of perfect esteeming rejection response.

F: Is there any kind of right-of-passage moment between mother and daughter in which mom teaches daughter how to reject Mr. Wrong with respect and dignity? Discuss the rejection lines you have ever used.

M: How do insincere rejection lines strike you? Do you know them when you hear them used?

JUST SAY IT

Today, some fifteen years after the Catholic singles group skit, I'm not only older but wiser. So the next time the words "I just got out of a bad relationship" begin to form on your tongue swallow them. We men know you're just not interested and besides, as a Christian you are called to a higher standard of esteeming honesty. But if not esteeming, we men will gladly settle for your honesty.

Your honesty is admitting to yourself that you just don't feel a drop of attraction or chemistry for this guy; your verbal answer to us, however, could be something like, "No, but thank you. I'm very flattered by your invitation. Tell me. Just out of curiosity why did you decide to ask *me* out?" That's it. Period!

Do you realize the beauty of asking not just that question but reflecting *any* question back at him? For one, that question gets his mind off the healthy and necessary dose of rejection he just suffered at the words of your mouth. Second, you expressed interest in knowing something about him. That's very flattering to men. Third, if you ask the question as I have written it above, you give him an opportunity to tell you what he's been wanting to confess to you for some time right there in the middle of your Christian singles group.

And after he inadequately replies with a stuttering stammer of superlative words, not to mention the deepest red-blushing face, you respond with your sweetest smile, "Oh, that's so sweet! Thank you."

Say nothing more. You are not expected to say anything more. Just look at him in the eyes until he changes the subject or makes his way back to the group of men huddled over the snack table.

F: Have you ever stayed and conversed with a man that you just rejected? What did it feel like? Maybe you simply just "escape" from the situation. How do you think a man feels when you run away immediately after he asks you out?

M: You're chatting with maybe Miss Right and things are going along smoothly. Then her friend comes up to her and pulls her by the arm saying, "We've got to get going right now!" or "There's someone over here that I want you to meet." What is your opinion of a woman who would let her friend disrupt the making of a potential love connection? What is your opinion of a woman who would use her friend as an escape strategy? Did you know that when you are talking one on one with a woman at your Christian singles group, her friends are periodically glancing over in her direction? They are looking for "rescue me" body language from the woman you're talking to. If she displays that, one of her friends will be right over to say, "Tiffany, there's someone over here I'd like you to meet." Are you aware that women do this behavior? What's your opinion of such women, both the one you're talking to and the one who pulled her away?

The Consequences of Saying It

The guy you reject as spelled out above will feel so elated by his "love" confession to you (i.e., the reasons why he asked you out, even if only the tip of his love-iceberg), that he will be walking tall for months until he interacts with a woman who inappropriately rejects him by saying, "I can't go out that night; I'll be shaving my back hair." But for you at the moment of his confession he will likely greet you from now on with a genuinely grateful smile.

You see, you esteemed him by rejecting him in the manner spelled out above. His nerves will settle down momentarily. And what about that invisible yet romantic thought balloon hovering above his head? Well, you just popped it good and plenty. Can you hear it wildly and erratically spirally down out of the air with a loud *eeeeEEEEeEeEEEEeeeeeEeeeeehhhhh* all the way down? Let that exhausted balloon plop to the ground. Once he sees it lying limp and flat on the floor the sting of your "No thank you," will begin to assuage, and he'll take on a fresh new perspective of you.

Despite the momentary sting of rejection, he will quickly put your name at the top of his list of women whose character he greatly and genuinely admires. He will be in such awe of your honest and compassionate forthrightness that he may start reviewing his circle of male friends to try and help you out finding a guy to whom you *are* attracted. Wouldn't you like to be surrounded by men with such a helpful attitude toward your finding Mr. Right? It's not that hard for women to do, but it does take guts and conviction. Now go back and memorize the rejection lines I have written for you above.

F: Have you ever made friends with a man that you
      rejected as a date? If not, why not? If so, what
      actions of yours led to friendship?
M: Once you've gotten the asking over with, is it easier
      to converse with the woman you just asked out but
      by whom you were rejected?

WHO'S GOT THE HARDER ROLE?

In my first two or three years of attending Christian singles group, I lamented the painful role of men as initiators of
dates. Indeed, my arguments were so well organized and communicated that most women also agreed with me. Those discussions always sparked fun debate. In short, men had it the
hardest because we had to face the possibility of rejection. The
women argued that *their* role was more precarious because
they felt they had no power or control or place to initiate a
date and thus had to suffer the "waiting game."

I sympathize with the plight of any woman who has to
wait on a man for him to make a decision to pursue or not to
pursue her. That is indeed the harder of the two roles in the
dating process. In general and on average, both men and
women must risk being rejected in order for a date between
them to come to fruition. The women must risk dropping
hints and the men must risk a follow-up to those hints with
charming conversation and an invitation to coffee. We simply
both have to surmount our fear of rejection or find some cop-
ing mechanism that washes our memory slate clean of fear
after rejection happens.

SHARON

I knew Sharon from grade school. We met again in college. She lived with a bunch of women in an off-campus house. There were at least six of them. I don't know how it was arranged, but I paid a planned visit to her in her house one weekday night. It happened to be girl's night in to watch their favorite sitcom or drama series.

I walked in and they were bunched up, on, and around the sofa parked in front of the TV. They were pretty much silent. I didn't have the confidence to make group conversation, and Sharon didn't make any gestures to excuse herself away from the room to talk with me. So I sat there quietly watching. One of the women was for some reason resting her arm on Sharon, a gesture that I was sure to be some kind of sisterhood type statement of unity. *"Whatever"*, I thought and just watched the show till the end. At the end Sharon walk-talked me away from the others and toward the small lobby area at the front door. We chatted ever so briefly, because as I remember it she just wasn't responding to my art of conversation.

A month or so later Christmas rolled by. We were both going to be home (I think I assumed that) between semesters, so I gave her a call a day or two after Christmas. I distinctly remember the psych-up exercise I performed before calling her. I grabbed an empty plastic gallon milk jug from my parent's kitchen trashcan, capped it, and took it out the back door. In the dark of the early evening where no one could see me, I proceeded to kick it around the backyard. The semi-loud "crack" as my foot hit it seemed to release some of the nervous tension I felt building up to the eventuality of the phone call.

The following scene is an amazingly similar portrayal many years later from the movie *Pride and Prejudice* (Dir. Joe Wright. Perf. Keira Knightley. Matthew Macfadyen. Brenda Blethyn. Donald Sutherland. Tom Hollander. Rosamund Pike. Jena Malone. Judi Dench. Focus Features, 2005). Mr. Bingley and Mr. Darcy left the Bennett home after completely botching their visit with the daughters. The two men retreated to the nearby woods. Mr. Bingley practiced his lines using Mr. Darcy as a stand-in for Jane. Do you remember Mr. Bingley's nervous pacing and utter frustration at his lack of ability to utter an intelligible sentence to even a mere stand-in-Jane?

By kicking the plastic milk container I was not expressing physical anger at Sharon; I was simply scolding myself through anger (much like Mr. Bingley did) over my own fear of pursuing Sharon, even though it was just by a simple phone call. I finally called her; she once again didn't respond to my art of conversation and so I left her alone after that.

Years later I attended a twenty-year high school reunion. I honestly wasn't thinking of seeing anyone in particular, but Sharon was there with her husband. There were about ten people in all that I was glad to see again.

Sharon's husband spent most of the time at the bar, which allowed us to have unfettered conversation. I was quite amazed at my awkward feelings as our eyes met periodically from across the room during the dinner. I fully didn't intend to even talk to her out of, I guess, the humiliation that I felt come back to me as if it were just last night that I was out back kicking around the empty gallon milk jug. Nevertheless, during the after-dinner socializing, she and another grade school classmate walked up to me and started chatting. The other woman left after a couple minutes, leaving me with Sharon. We chatted superficially; I didn't know what to say beyond the usual how long have you been married and how many kids do you have?

She unexpectedly blurted out, "You know in grade school I had the biggest crush on you." At that time I was completely unaware of her feelings.

I wish I had a camcorder focused on me at that moment. I am very rarely both fully spontaneously emotional and expressive. I said to her, "What? You had a crush on me? I pursued you in college! Don't you remember? I called you and even visited you in that house with your college friends! You didn't respond. How can you say that you had a crush on me? What else was I supposed to do?"

I felt like grabbing her by the shoulders (but I didn't) and shaking some sense into her during my response.

She said, "I know! I know! I knew you were pursuing me at that time, but I was just going through a weird phase in my life." In Sharon's defense two or three years prior to my Christmas time phone call, her family experienced tragedy. Surely she had more things on her mind than making pleasant small talk with me on the phone. Surely it was unlikely that she wanted to make her life even more difficult at that time with thoughts of a romantic relationship.

So what's the point of this story? The point is to demonstrate that even when a woman feels attraction for a guy she may inadvertently rebuff his pursuit efforts. Who can predict the way a woman will react to a man's invitation that she might even want to accept? After all, she may have a history of getting burned by a boy while testing the waters of romance starting from childhood. Those memories might derail any feelings of interest she might otherwise have in Mr. Right's invitation.

Can you see how it becomes less and less appealing for a guy to approach a woman cold-turkey? When a woman drops hints, a man usually detects them. He subconsciously concludes that she is giving him the green light to kick into pursuit mode. The woman's part is done; the man's part has just begun. The small gestures, in the form of hints, that a woman emits is an investment in a future husband who will live his life time pursuing you in a committed marriage. All that is required of women is a small spark in the form of a subtle hint to electrify his romantic pursuit mode.

CHAPTER 12

IT'S ONLY NATURAL

THE PINK PANTHER

I remember this line from one of my favorite childhood Saturday morning cartoons. The Pink Panther in the cartoon was successful at outwitting the police detective always trying to solve crimes (*The Pink Panther*, by DePatie-Freleng Enterprises. Dir. Friz Freleng, circa 1964, NBC circa 1969). Pink Panther, however, NEVER spoke. He was all about body language and facial expressions.

At the end of one particular episode ("Sink Pink". 1965), however, the Pink Panther finally opened his mouth and said in a British accent, "Why can't men be more like animals?"

I wasn't sure what he meant at the time, but I think I do now. If men were to rely more on their instincts as opposed to their calculations, then they would be more successful at relationships. Let's review instinctive courtship behavior among animals.

ANIMALS KNOW THE DANCE

You don't have to look too far for examples of animal courtship behavior. As far as I have observed there are some universalities from species to species.

First and foremost the male ALWAYS makes the initial approach to the female. After the male performs some tests using his physical senses, he advances his efforts for physical contact. The next universality is that the female will rebuff the male's advances. Her rejection behavior can be walking away like pigeons, turning away from the male like grazing cows or outright snarling and showing of sharp teeth like dogs. Yet the male in all species doesn't usually give up; he is persistent through to the end. Those two simple universalities will suffice for my argument.

To summarize, the male initiates and the female rebuffs him, yet the male does not give up till he wears the female down, and immediately afterward, the minute or two-long courtship is consummated.

A similar courtship dance is performed among humans. Okay, don't get morally grossed out. For good Christian men, the "consummation" of their efforts to wear you down is simply getting you to agree to meet them for coffee. For the purposes of this book that's where my analogy ends between humans and lower animals.

The Point Of Pink Panther's Question

Do Christian women expect men to be relentless in their efforts to wear them down? Not only do they refrain from giving men hints of their interest they may also actively rebuff men's advances. Isn't this rebuffing behavior reminiscent of what goes on in the animal world? But don't take that as an insult; after all, humans are animals, just animals with higher mental, emotional, spiritual, etc., functions.

As I conceded in another chapter, having this "Mr. Brave" expectation of men can work for you. But once again you had better be sure you have the animal magnetism that will attract the type of man you secretly desire. Otherwise you may end up a confirmed bachelorette for life.

WALT DISNEY CAN TEACH WOMEN A THING OR TWO

Have you seen the animated movie *Bambi*? (Prod. Walt Disney. Animated Movie. Dist. RKO Radio Pictures. 1942). It's been a long time since I've seen it that I don't remember much of it, except a forest fire and talking animals. One day I was home visiting my parents along with my mom's fifty-five-year-old cousin, Gregg. Somehow our conversation incorporated the word "twitter-pated."

Gregg asked, "What does that mean?"

My dad gave a look of surprise. "You don't know what twitter-pated means? Well, I have the DVD of Bambi. Let me play it for you." At my strong suggestion my dad agreed to skip to the part of the film that defines "twitter-pated."

Maybe you remember the scene. The wise old owl is sitting in the tree looking down on Bambi, the male deer, Thumper, the male rabbit and Flower, the male skunk. These three characters were snickering about the behavior of another male animal in the presence of a female of his own species. The owl commented, "He's just twitter-pated."

All three animals in unison responded, "Huh? Twitter-pated? What's that?"

The wise old owl proceeded to describe a male's reaction to a pretty female at the dawn of the spring when he has reached sexual maturity.

What Walt portrays in this scene is the natural order of things. Being at the dawn of sexual maturity themselves, the three characters denied ever having such feelings for "her" and went on their way together. One by one each of the three characters met up with a female of their kind and got the twitter-pated feelings and left the other boys for the girl.

What's the point? In the movie the three new adult males were pretty much walking together as if invincible to this twitter-pated phenomenon. They were quite unaware of the presence of any females. However, the females took it upon themselves to do something to attract the attention of the invincible males.

And *that's* the point! The females *did* something to attract the attention of the males. Without the action of the females, the males would have simply walked by, unaware of their presence.

Now for the male audience of this book: Once a woman has intentionally attracted your attention it's your turn. *Say something to her!*

And so my book boils down to two simple sentences. For the women: "Do something—drop a hint!" And for the men: "Do something—follow up the hint!"

An Inaccurate Analogy, After All

And now for a confession. Admittedly there's a huge flaw in my analogy between animal and human courtship behavior. I falsely gave you the impression that female animals do nothing to encourage the advances of males. That's not true.

As the Pink Panther suggested, animals are driven by their instinct, which is influenced by their physical senses. When a female animal is receptive to mating, she will emit a pheromone, a scent that the male, in some species, can detect from miles away. If you own an unspayed female cat or dog you know what I'm talking about. You know about the periodic visits from male cats or dogs to your front door. These persistent visitors can be annoying at best, but downright vicious when they can't connect the scent with the physical contact of your female pet.

I distinctly remember an incident of a stray male dog showing up in my childhood neighborhood. He wouldn't leave, so the dogcatchers were called in. The dog kicked into survival mode as he realized the purpose of the noose that was stretched out to him at the end of a long metal pole. The dog obviously didn't want to leave the vicinity of my neighbor's house. I knew at that time that the female dog living there was not spayed.

So in my description, despite the rebuffing behavior on the part of a female animal, her body chemistry signals that she is reproductively most receptive. In other words, when the female dog is in heat, she gives the male a physical sign—a scent—that she is receptive. It is a clear and unmistakable sign to the male. As such, despite her rebuffing behavior—snarling, show of teeth—the male knows she will ultimately yield to his advances once he wears her down. Without her physical sign, the male dog would probably be off somewhere else, front-paw rummaging through an open trash can or digging up secretly buried bones.

Does this uninspired behavior sound like some guys you know? At your Christian singles group, are the guys constantly huddled around the snack table? Or are they constantly huddled around a conversation centered on football, baseball, or basketball? If they start discussing the finer points of synchronized swimming, don't worry. There's still hope.

What can you do about it? Plenty! You just have to minimize men's fear of rejection. Your physical sign to get a man's jets lit is dropping him a hint. Want to see some male animal behavior cloaked in well-polished social etiquette? Drop a man a hint. But again, please, don't do it just to see a man react: That would be mean.

TAKE THE BEES, FOR EXAMPLE: A LECTURE FOR WOMEN

I know that drawing analogies between the mating behavior of lower animal's and human's courtship behaviors might not be the most effective way of convincing women to drop subtle hints. As such what follows is another analogy albeit less graphic and more artful.

There's a great analogy in the flower-pollinating behavior of bees. Bees (men) buzz around flowers (woman) because flowers have nectar that the bees collect and transport back to the comb to store as honey. The flowers need the bees because the bees knock pollen off of the part of the flower called the stamen. The loose pollen falling off the stamen and onto the part of the flower called the pistol acts to fertilize the flower leading to seed formation. Such seeds can then be planted to make more flowering plants. In early spring, growing flower plants send out buds that will eventually open to become flowers. Once open, the bees can do their nectar-gathering thing while incidentally fertilizing the flowers with the flower's own pollen. Hence, the circle of life.

What follows is a similar animated story I just made up. You can tell it to your niece at an age-appropriate time. The story is geared for children but the message is for you too. Try and read it from the viewpoint of your inner child.

Imagine that flowers and bees can talk. One spring morning a flowering plant named Rose Bud wakes up and asks, "I wonder if Mr. Bee will visit and pollinate me today." All the while it is too early in spring and Rose only has buds at this point. No blooms.

Meanwhile Mr. Bee is hanging out in the comb doing his worker thing in preparation for all the nectar that he and his fellow bees will be soon bringing back from the flowers. Every once in a while the bees look out of the comb to see if the buds have bloomed into flowers. The designated lookout bee reports, "Not yet!" and all the bees groan with disappointment and continue working.

This series of events transpires every day as the days become longer and the sun splashes the earth to a fertile warm. But Rose Bud is a bit of a transplant. Long ago her mother's pollen was blown from the original plot of ground where all of her family still grows. Momma Rose never got to tell Rose Bud how to attract Mr. Bee. Now Rose Bud grows among other flowers that look quite different from her. Because of their long history in this neck of the woods once they bloom her foster family will enjoy the security of having many Mr. Bees visit them daily. Rose Bud, however, will not. (Uh-oh. I feel a song coming on.) The other bloomed flowers gather around lonely Rose Bud and console her by singing,

"Open your bud, Rose.
Open your bud, Rose.
If you're gonna' pollinate,
You've got to open your bud, Rose."

So by the end of the song, which includes much choreo-graphed dancing, Rose Bud realizes she has to bloom before Mr. Bee will give her his pollination attention. Rose Bud finally opens her bloom and sure enough several Mr. Bees vie for her nectar. Her neighboring flowers give out a cheer and decide that she can now legitimately be called Rose Bloom just like her mom. Rose Bloom goes on to produce pollen happily ever after. The end.

Have I insulted your intelligence? Maybe that's a good thing if doing so helps you to remember the take-home message. If you are going to attract Mr. Bee you've got to open your rose bud and bloom. The bee will take care of the rest. Just as a bloom is a flower's invitation to a bee a hint is a woman's invitation to a man. That's the take-home message.

If you still wish to hang on to a fanciful expectation that a man is going to approach you without your hint, you can close this book now because I can offer nothing more to change your mind. Put my book down and go pick up your romance novel and your daytime soap operas. But don't be discouraged. Like I said before, some women are attractive enough not to have to give hints. The downside is that it's not always going to be your Mr. Musing that approaches you uninvited. Also you had better be sure you are all-that-and-a-bag-of-chips-worth-it and can afford not to give hints or you will end up a confirmed bachelorette for life.

Dropping hints is not an easy role for women. If you are finally convinced that dropping hints works you'll want to know *why* it works. What deep longing in men is met by a woman's subtle hint (other than minimizing fear of rejection)?

Most importantly there is an innate desire in a man to pursue not just a woman but anything he wants and/or needs. Engaging in pursuit mode makes him feel manly; in a sense he needs to pursue something in order to express and fulfill those leftover pursuit desires found in cavemen. As such, a man's actual pursuit of you is a joy and pleasurable to him. But if this joy is tainted in any way with feelings of self-doubt and fear that accompany thoughts of rejection, he will run away yelping like a dog with tail between legs.

To conclude, just as a flower in bloom is an invitation to a bee, a woman's hint is an invitation to a man. Without your invitation, there is in general not going to be a response from the man. If your hint includes using my enumerated suggestions (see Chapter 5: HUMAN EQUIVALENT OF PHEROMONES, THE HINTS), most men will recognize them as such if only at the subconscious level. I believe that the feeling that a woman receives by being pursued by the man of her liking is a God-given religious experience, one that fulfills her emotionally the same way pursuit mode fulfills a man. So why are you depriving yourself from the feeling of being pursued? If the expression is true that if you want to attract bees just put out some honey then your hint is honey to men.

CHAPTER 13

THE BIG BAD WOLF WANTS IN

Knock, Knock...Who's There?

This chapter focuses on media influence and how it constantly knocks on the door of women's psyche. There is no greater example of media influence on women's psyche than cigarette ads from the 1960's and 1970's.

Looking back on old magazine ads and TV commercials, I say to myself, "If they aired that ad today with that claim it would be a joke." Cigarette advertisements offered the smoker a sense of elite social status, a certain air of coolness, an unearned power to influencing people's perception of the smoker and, oh yes, *satisfaction*. Aside from the pharmacological effects of the inhaled nicotine on the addicted smoker, I don't know what is meant by "satisfaction." In the 1960s, however, there was no mention of the health risks associated with smoking.

Thankfully what's come a long way, baby, is the Food and Drug Administration (FDA) in its mandatory warnings placed on cigarette packages. History will never forget the testimony by David Kessler (Commissioner of FDA circa 1990–1997) before a federal subcommittee, followed shortly thereafter by the top seven perjuring tobacco executives of their respective cigarette-producing corporations. Dr. Kessler's subsequent book is a powerful and candid look into our government's intentionally negligent attitude toward cigarette manufacturers (Kessler, David. *A Question of Intent: A Great American*

171

Battle with a Deadly Industry. New York. Public Affairs, 2001).

Sales tax on tobacco products nets the government lots of spending revenue. The money is spent on earmarks, pork projects and other programs that will ostensibly benefit the public far more than banning deadly cigarettes. So if you are like me you are baffled by the legal sales and easy availability of cigarettes. To understand it you just have to follow the money trail back to the very government that both investigated and regulates big tobacco practices and continues to be dependent on cigarette sales tax. I call it classic conflict of interest over which, sadly, no one gets conflicted anymore.

The straw that broke Joe Camel's back (officially *Old Joe* the iconic cartoon character once splashed on the packages of the Camel brand cigarettes promoted by R.J. Reynolds from 1987 to 1997 allegedly targeting children) was perhaps the Regulation of Tobacco Products House Committee Hearing on Energy and Commerce Subcommittee on Health and the Environment of April 14, 1994. This hearing was lead by two heroic men: Henry Waxman (D-CA) and Ron Wyden (D-Oregon). You can view the top seven tobacco company executives (including William Campbell, President & CEO, Philip Morris, USA; James W. Johnston, Chairman and CEO, RJR Tobacco Company; Joseph Taddeo, President, U.S. Tobacco Company; Andrew H. Tisch, Chairman and CEO, Lorillard Tobacco Company; Edward A. Horrigan, Chairman and CEO, Liggett Group, Inc.; Thomas E. Sandefur, Chairman and CEO, Brown and Williamson Tobacco Corp.; Donald S. Johnston, President and CEO, American Tobacco Company) perjuring themselves at this video link http://senate.ucsf.edu/tobacco/executives1994congress.html. Their collective statement was, "I believe that nicotine (in cigarettes) is *not* addictive."

Not surprising was the finding that nicotine levels were being genetically manipulated to increase concentrations in tobacco plants to more quickly and surely hook more smokers. I recently saw one article, which suggested that nicotine levels were being manipulated as late as 2006 more than ten years after the infamous hearing!

What's that got to do with the title of this section? Cigarette advertising *is* who was knocking on the door of American's mind and soul in those ads. As a society since we didn't know much about the effects of cigarette smoke on the body (as if that weren't painfully obvious by the body's reaction to its first full inhale) we could only answer, "Who's there?" and have to believe who the cigarette companies said they were (purveyor of perceived social status, cool, and satisfaction).

But here's the main question: What advertisements today are knocking on the door of women's minds and souls that purvey goods or services that are simply toxic to their hearts and attitudes? Will people in their twenties in the year 2040 look at ads from today and say, "No wonder single people in their fifties, sixties . . . have been single all their lives. They bought into those screwball ads."

The problem is that it's kind of hard to recognize screwball ads in the year they are produced. They are typically very acutely, socially relevant. Often times they dictate future social trends and instill life style expectations. Thus, hindsight is 20/20.

But it's important for we Christians to be discerning about cultural influences. Now I can't list a bunch of ads/products that should be avoided because I don't have 20/20. But let me ask you this what-if question. Scenario: You are invited to speak at career day for a local junior high school. You have been working after college for five years in a reputable company revered for it's just treatment of employees and its benefits to the local community. Even the kids you're about to speak to want to work there eventually.

What if you said to the kids, "Getting your college education is so important for your future. I personally aspired to become college educated for the sole purpose of bettering my mind and increasing my knowledge in a subject that I really enjoy. My college degree also made me eligible for the job that I now have. Yet I can't wait for the day that I meet Mr. Right, get married, quit my job, and be a stay-at-home mom to raise my kids. I know as a one-income family we will have to sacrifice many luxuries that have become the norm in our culture. But to me, being at home to raise my kids is the most important thing in the world to me and presumably my future husband and God." In your imagination do you see the faces of the girls in your audience? Have their jaws dropped down in unbelief? As you read this section did *your* jaw drop in unbelief?

Let's explore your jaw, your reflex reaction, just a bit more. Did what I just write seem antiquated and outdated for our socially advanced culture today? Does it seem ludicrous for a college-educated woman to aspire to quit her job to stay home and raise her kids? Does it seem like a financial mistake in the long run to eschew a second household income just to stay home and raise children? Have you bought into the advertised lifestyle of the double income family and the larger-than-necessary home, more luxurious than necessary second car, kitchen full of all the latest gadgets from QVC channel on and on and on? The irony is that even with double incomes many families still struggle to afford it all! While it's true that you may also struggle in a one-income household at least you'll be at your modest home with your modest lifestyle and your well-indoctrinated kids.

Going back to career day. Of course it's important for women to prepare for a career. For one they may never get married, because they were too busy or proud to read this book, and will therefore have to take care of themselves. Second, even in marriage there is no guarantee of children due to biological infertility (ironically quite possibly due to the stress of full time careers), and divorce is a 50 percent likelihood. Third, after the nest is empty a woman may want to continue in her career where she left off. Fourth, maybe it will be the husband that forgoes a career and stays home with the kids while the wife works.

But the question I have for you is the following. Is your undivided attention on forging a career obscuring your vision of the eligible men around you? Instead of your body language being rich with subtle hint dropping does it inadvertently announce to good men "Don't even think about it, buddy!"?

There would be men out there saying, "Knock, knock" to you, but to us it appears that you are not "home" to answer the door. Humorously, men are often accused of being emotionally unavailable; I hereby assert that women are often knock-knock unavailable.

So thanks to the equal rights movement of the sixties, seventies, and continuing still today, women are a very strong presence in the out-of-the-home career world. I'm trying to wrap up this section, but I keep having more and more thoughts to add. Recently it was reported on the news that women are now more than half of matriculated college students. Moreover, women are in a better position to move up the C*O ladder. We still have the salary disparity to solve but the progress trajectory is clearly heading in that direction. All that said women are now full of choices regarding "what to do with my life."

So tell me, are you happy with your career choice so far? Have you yet accepted that there are many, many more workers in your company than positions into which you might advance? Are you a contender for one of those highly sought-after positions? Statistically speaking, probably not or until someone older retires.

Thus, have you looked twenty, thirty, even forty years into the future to see yourself doing exactly what you are doing now? Perhaps the product changes and the supporting technology changes but your basic contribution to the assembly line of product output remains the same. If you've been brave enough to look that far, then you see what most men eventually call "my portion" in life. Of course a man's humble acceptance of his grim career reality is the aftermath of a midlife crisis in which he looks twenty, thirty . . . years into the future to see himself doing exactly what he is doing now. You are not immune to the same midlife crisis.

There is a major difference, however, between single men and single women having a midlife crisis. A single man in his forties begins to accept the reality that maybe the Lord does not have a wife and/or children in his future. And without a wife there are no children unless he adopts kids as a single parent. Thus his job is viewed as a vehicle to get him to retirement and not much else. Top that off with an uninspiring job and you basically get a pretty moody male for a few years.

Women on the other hand are not dependent on men for children. There are ways they can completely circumvent male relationships to become pregnant (artificial insemination, seducing an unsuspecting man, for example). Women have to play the waiting game for marriage but they do have a choice in the matter of bearing children and having a single family. A single woman in the midst of a midlife crisis can remedy her "portion" in life by finally having children one way or another. Her uninspiring career suddenly has new meaning; it helps her afford the truly meaningful aspect of her existence, her children.

I do believe that men and women alike embark on a career in their early twenties with pie-in-the-sky dreams of a "power" career. We both eschew marriage and family until we see how a career plays out. Then our early forties hits us like a ton of bricks. And we ask ourselves, "What fruits do I have to show for my career efforts?" And what if we put off marriage and family in favor of harvesting those fruits? Are you satisfied with how you have chosen to act upon your equal rights? What fruits did it net you? Did you "equal right" yourself into a childless bachelorette hood? Oh, sister, what have you done?

This section is admittedly hard-hitting for women. Not so much for men because we don't have to reconcile not having children in favor of career efforts. We know we can't have children on our own like women can. Bearing your own bio children may be too late for some of you. But it's not too late for marriage and possibly adoption (although couples over forty may not qualify for infant adoption due to their age).

For some of you in your twenties, *now* is the time to decide what is most important to you as a Christian woman. Maybe it would help to have you imagine that your career turns out to be like 95 percent of most people's in this country: boring, routine, non-stimulating, unfulfilling but it pays the bills. What then would you turn to, to give your life meaning? For some the answer might mean serving the poor in a developing nation. But for most of you I suspect that it means marriage and family. Are you investing in the men around you as much as you are investing in your career? If not, I recommend that you start by dropping hints. It could be that simple. That's the main solution to singleness, a message scattered throughout this book ad nausea.

Finally, to wrap up this section, I ask you the following question. The Equal Rights Amendment says to you, "Knock knock!" You already know who's there. So tell me, after all the "ERA advertising" over the past fifty years what is your take on what it has to offer you? Do you buy into its advertising like so many did and still do buy into the cigarette smoking mystique? The next section will help you find your answer (each person's answer will be different).

EVALUATION TIME

No one likes to be evaluated. Don't worry; this section is more of a self-evaluation. Imagine yourself very old and facing God as you approach the pearly gates of heaven. God asks, "Precious son/daughter, what do you bring me?" Fill in the following blanks as an exercise.

I, (your name here)_____ used my mental blessings to earn a degree in _____. I advanced to a career title of _____. My employer and I contributed to helping others by producing these goods/services _____. In my free time I accomplished_____

_____.
Regarding   marriage   and   family   I

_____.

Regarding my relationships I _____
_____.

Regarding my witness to others about You and Your son Jesus I_____

_____.

Now imagine that God is holding a weighing balance consisting of two pans dangling from the ends of a cross bar. On the left pan you place all of your God-glorifying answers from the above blanks with the exception of one of those blanks. Place your answer to the final statement "regarding marriage and family I" on the right pan. You are likely single since you're reading this book. As such God would be glorified by your life if the left pan is overloaded with your God-glorifying life and slams the pan down to the table.

Meanwhile the right pan holding your marriage/family accomplishments which is empty presents no counter weight to the left pan. But what if all your left-hand pan answers are not God-glorifying and in reality you simply led a very selfish, survival-based material existence? With nothing God-glorifying in the left pan and no marriage/family on the right pan the scale is balanced basically with nothing on either side.

With nothing on either side of the scale your response to God's question, "What do you bring me?" is, well, *nothing.* Now I'm not making a statement about works or faith-based path of being a Christian. I'm just provoking you to think beyond making ends meet here on earth and what you are doing to further the Kingdom of God.

The above topics for your response can all be summed up into one question. What is it about your life and how you spend your existence that is so God-glorifying that you had no time or energy to drop hints? Some of my readers will have many God-glorifying "weights" to add to their left scale pan while I suspect many more will have none. If you have no weights on either left or right pan how do you explain this lack of "fruit" in your life? Who is knocking on your door and whom are you letting in to your life that's distracting you from dropping hints?

EMASCULATING MEN...MORE THROWING OUT THE BABY?

Who's knocking at men's doors? Here's a quote from a book I read by a popular Christian author. "Walk into most churches in America, have a look around, and ask yourself this question: What is a Christian man? Don't listen to what is said, look at what you find there. There is no doubt about it. You'd have to admit a Christian man is . . . bored." (Eldredge, John. *Wild at Heart, Discovering the Secret of a Man's Soul.* Nashville: Thomas Nelson, Inc., 2001) 7.

That one sentence confirmed much of how I was feeling, as I was nearly eight years in the Christian church. I couldn't place my finger on it, but there was something gnawing at my psyche. It wasn't that the men around me were all touchy-feely; I happen to enjoy expressing joy and care for certain people that way. But what bugged me, even today, is the lack of a sense of action from my fellow Christian men.

This feeling was succinctly summed up for me when I scanned the congregation during a recent church service. I asked myself, "Would any of the fathers I see here support or take pride in their son's decision to enlist in the armed services, if necessary, to protect our nation?" This question encapsulates my gut full of feelings on the issue of the Christian church emasculating its men.

The Bible emphasizes the male as head of the household and spiritual leader over his family, including his wife. Now I don't have any children to know firsthand, but the leadership of a family and a wife must be a big responsibility. I cannot speak highly enough of men in this role. But there must be something more to being a Christian man than this. I don't quite know what it is; it's mostly just a gut feeling.

Take the following question. The Bible also emphasizes the importance of the body of Christ being made up of many parts, like a community is made up of many families. Imagine your church community as a representative sample of all churches across this nation. Do you as a woman feel that men drawn from your church community can keep your neighborhood and your country safe? Would they step up to the job if they saw it necessary to do so? How about if a mad gunman disrupts your church service? Would the men in attendance take decisive action against him like a mother bear would selflessly defend her cubs? How many men in your church community have careers in law enforcement, daily putting their lives in the line of fire for the sake of our nation's domestic tranquility? How many Christian churches actually prepare men for selfless and decisive action such as the men who successfully foiled the one highjacker's plans by storming the cockpit on 9/11?

Let's face it. The emasculating of the Christian men in our community has the overall result of making them utterly content with praying away confrontational type situations. And the only reason why they get away with such hand washing is because there are Rambo types outside the Christian Church to do the difficult duty of confrontation for them. Don't get me wrong. Prayer is powerful but not when it's used to hide behind the necessity of taking action.

Turning the other cheek, by the way, can also be abused as a place to hide away from taking action. Our interpretation of Scripture also contributes to muddling men's role in taking decisive action against our enemies. "Love your enemies, turn the other cheek, if a robber takes your belongings give him your coat as well" are such sticking points. I have to admit that I don't know the cultural context in which those verses were first recorded.

To conclude I guess I can't stop you from thinking that the only way I assess the masculinity factor among church men is by whether or not they will fight to protect the body of Christ, their community and our nation. Well, given the above examples I can't blame you. Here's another try. My proposal to start a volleyball outreach at a church was rejected. The outreach pastor in essence argued, "Sports often times brings out men's sinful competitive nature; we are not set up at this time to handle such issues as they arise." What a disgrace! It's no wonder why there are far more women in the Christian church than men.

What are churches doing to reach out to men in your community? Does it host activities such as sports outreach or fun labor-based activities like Habitat for Humanity house building, a garage for auto repairs, a weight-lifting room, or a team of men who volunteers to do small household repairs for single moms or the elderly? Here's a clever one. What if churches were to become leaders at organizing men into neighborhood watch groups? Isn't that an excellent venue for outreach to men? Imagine a church setting up a semi-challenging but fun obstacle course in its own backyard for group competition. It would serve the purpose of outreach for men in the local community appealing to their desire to be part of the community in which they live and to learn to be decisive and active in safety-threatening situations. The physical training aspect of it can lead to the camaraderie experienced in boot camp, on a football team, and in police and fire departments for example.

This outreach idea is genius! What other activity can better give a man the sense that he is protecting his community, getting some semi-challenging physical activity, standing out as one belonging to a network of men in his community and, dare I say, forming healthy Christian relationships with men from the sponsoring church? Can you feel the incredibly healthy boost to a man's psyche that such purposefulness and belongingness can foster? Furthermore, can you see how a man's boosted psyche and sense of belonging will bring him back to these relationships again and again? And if there is a core group of Christian men from their local church hosting the program, it's just another step away from exposing the other men to the Gospel. So tell me, don't such men of decisiveness and action appeal to you as men by whom you would like to be asked out, friends, courted or married?

Now that I have painted such a picture of Christian men with a healthy male vibrato take a look back at your own congregation and tell me how many men there fit that picture. How many of them are single? How many will tolerate the emasculating influence that they are subconsciously feeling in their soul? How many are unfairly labeled as having questionable Christian character as a result of not portraying an unusually sensitive male? As you have probably already surmised, the chances are bleak that you will find a man of decisiveness and action in your church. Such men of action are the modern day version of a knight in shining armor.

Armor, unfortunately, is frowned upon in modern day churches. In one section (Chapter 6: HE'S MR. BRAVE BUT CAN HE LEARN?) I write about a man asking out women who are not hinting to him. On the surface women might view him as brave and courageous. But I see him as trying something over and over again that's not working and expecting different results the next time he tries. Remember this is part of the definition of insanity. Because passing on the genes for learning and adapting are criteria for having smarter children, you want to avoid guys like that. Also if there is some genetic component underlying docile and emasculated men, it is unlikely to be passed on to children because these men won't attract women. If you're a single woman, no doubt, you feel that your church is full of such men.

To conclude, it is secular society sneaking into Christian churches and knocking at the door of women. The main impact from the Equal Rights Movement is equal opportunity for women and less dependence on men. A secondary impact is men learning to be more sensitive to those rights. Moreover, men extrapolate from what secular society expects and bring their "sensified" behavior into the church. Such sensified behavior is affirmed in the expectations and teachings of the Christian church. For Christian men, therefore, the Christian church itself is part of the influence knocking at their door insisting on male sensitivity that sadly shows up as passivity. It's a double dose of emasculation, in some ways for the better, some for the worse.

A common complaint from Christian women about Christian men is that the men are too passive, not aggressive enough. Now you know why that is. Christian women must realize that men who don't ask out women cold-turkey or don't pursue them despite their rebuffing behavior are simply conforming to both secular and Christian expectations of sensitivity toward women. It is far easier to teach or empower women to drop hints to men than it is to teach men to be insensitive about their approach to asking women out. Hence, there is a need for women to drop hints.

F: If the men in your church were more aggressive with their approach towards asking out women would that somehow be an attractive force leading you to see them as more desirable and lead you to naturally drop hints?

THE RULES

In the HEAR ME ROAR section (Chapter 3), I included some pithy phrases conveying a fictional composite attitude of Miss Liberated. I'm sure I left out some good ones but those included will suffice. Miss Liberated brings to mind a woman's book. The essence of this book appears to be that you make yourself out to be more desirable, interesting, mysterious and harder-to-get than you actually are in order to attract a man. Here's one quote that supports this notion:

"That's the secret: you act as if everything's great, even if you're on the verge of flunking college or getting fired. You walk briskly, as if you know where you're going, which is just around the room. You keep moving. You don't stand in a corner waiting for anyone. They (men) have to catch you in motion." (Fein and Schneider. *The Rules, Time-tested Secrets for Capturing the Heart of Mr. Right*. New York: Warner Books, Inc., 1995) 24.

Do you see how a man going through Miss Rule's mental...stuff will collapse (or worse) after finally marrying her? Can you hear yourself woefully complaining, "He used to be so romantic before we got married."? I wrote "collapse (or worse)" because what if your new husband learns quickly by being married to you that you are simply as plain as plain Jane gets? Are you really "all that and so much more"? You had better be because a man's disillusionment over his new wife can be scary. Instead of playing hard-to-get with a nose in the air attitude, it's best to simply drop hints to attract the man of your choice and let him take care of the rest.

Here's a case in point. Rulinda conducted her church superficial relationships according to "the rules." Well, I mean not her biblical conduct, just how she socialized with men. After a service or singles gathering, she would bounce from one person to the next, spending not more than a minute with a man. She was the one who got me to read "the rules." Rulinda was college-educated but quite ordinary in her hobbies. That is, she didn't have any. I learned that part of the rules was to cast an illusion about yourself that makes you look more interesting, more popular, more intriguing. In short, she was good at it. I told her one-day that once a woman lets a guy into her life, he will see what she is really made of. It won't be a happy ending when that little balloon of illusion in his mind pops from the reality check prick of who you really are.

Here's where it gets a bit complicated. In my view "the rules" and dropping hints are not mutually exclusive. I might get some hate mail from males for writing this, but here goes because I truly believe it. Yes, go ahead and play by the "rules." But don't forget to drop your subtle hints. In this day and age we men have already learned to ignore the girls who play the rules head games; that is, we men look the other way and move on in order not to be labeled a stalker. Indeed we men are dumb in this area; we don't know when to pursue romantically or when to step away from the girl. As it turns out a man is a stalker or a romancer simply based on the woman's level of attraction for him. I covered that concept in another chapter (Chapter 6, I'VE BEEN SCOOPED and UNTITLED FOR A REASON). Anyway, "the rules" only work for supermodels.

Combine the rules with subtle hints. These two behaviors will drive a guy crazy for you or count you off as psychotic. It all depends on how you play it. For example, you bait him with a subtle hint, a clear smile, or one of the other many subtle hints listed in another chapter (Chapter 5: HUMAN EQUIVALENT OF PHEROMONES: THE HINTS). In response to your consistent hints (no telling how many weeks or months this will take), he will start to single you out with the intention of asking you out. After all, you gave him a hint.

But then you play the rules to rebuff him a bit. Then he'll think you're just friendly like that with all the guys, even the socially awkward. But you drop another hint, and he'll be confused, especially after he observes you and sees that you don't drop hints to just anyone. So he pursues you again after you hint to him again. You rebuff him a second time. He gets agitated. This cycle plays out until you can't stand not having his attention. After all he is charming and witty. Alternatively he might focus his attention on somebody else.

Entering this game will take keen discernment on your part to know when is the right time to let him in for coffee. Too soon and you don't play by the rules and ostensibly lose his interest; too late and you just might earn yourself a nifty reputation as a cold-hearted woman who likes to lead men on just to see them crash after you toy with his attention.

Sounds both complicated and simple at the same time. But let's think about it for a moment. Do you want to be so premeditated? Don't you just want to enjoy the force of nature and where ever it may take you? Of course you do. Besides, how does the force of the Holy Spirit factor in to all of your little rules and all that premeditated manipulation of men? I think not at all. And what about living your life in the freedom of God's grace? Sure, your life is going to be filled with challenges from the Lord, challenges that build your character.

Nevertheless, your life is full of grace, and you are filled with the joy of the Lord. All you simply need to do is let that joy of the Lord overflow in the direction of the man that you like. That man will take care of the rest. Doesn't that natural plan sound ridiculously simple and spiritually in-sync with God's plan of natural attraction between men and women? Why confuse that plan for you with "the rules"?

Conclusions About "The Rules"

In conclusion, women's reaction to the equal rights movement has ironically destroyed the very ingredient in them that attracts men: *vulnerability* (notice that I didn't say that the movement itself destroyed the ingredient). You might be throwing your hands up in frustration right now shouting, "But that's what the last thirty years have been all about: growing less dependent on men and therefore more self-sufficient, less needy!" But I say to you that while I agree with you I should underscore that vulnerability has nothing to do with need or dependency; vulnerability is a language of passion and romance. And this kind of vulnerability is sweetly expressed in a woman's hint.

Perhaps a better source for learning the difference between neediness and vulnerability can be found in the women living in retirement homes across this nation. On the topic of the last thirty years, those retired women might tell you that "You've thrown the baby out with the bathwater." To be clear, women have thrown out their emitted aphrodisiac of vulnerability (the baby) with dependence on men (the bathwater).

Admittedly I am attracted to women who take advantage of their opportunities, especially their academic opportunities. In my dating experience, I learned that being equally yoked (or close to it) educationally is an important value to me. Also, I appreciate that women with a college degree have much protection against the tyranny that men have historically exerted in single-income households. As such, tyranny and ignorance are also part of the bathwater that is being thrown out. Happily, however, the baby of vulnerability is always with you. You just have to take it out for a stroll on a regular basis. Ahem . . . to be clear, the stroll would be dropping hints.

There is no use for "the rules" of a modern day Christian woman. But let me be painfully clear. While you await a response from the hints that you drop, it is critical in this present age to earn your college degree and embark on a career. Even if Mr. Musing responds to you before you finish your degree, completing school should be an agreed part of your immediate future. I stress this first and foremost for the mental benefits of a college education and second so that you are of high competitive value to a prospective employer. As such you will not be forced to endure an abusive marriage just because you can't afford to leave it. Also, *you* may be the one to work and your husband may end up being a stay-at-home dad. I'll bet the pioneering women of the equal rights movement never imagined that they were paving the way for modern day women to carry the responsibility of kids and stay-at-home dad. Now *that's* getting closer to true equality! How do ya' like them ERA apples?

HEAR ME BACK OFF

Men have changed in two major ways in response to the women's equal rights movement. 1) Men have increased their sensitivity toward women in the workplace, giving them equal esteem and opportunity as equal colleagues, not just as women. 2) Men have learned to become hypersensitive about their approach to asking women out on dates (especially at work) and their manner of pursuit for women. We men want to avoid at all costs having our romantic pursuit behavior be misconstrued as stalking behavior. Men fear an unfair reputation of being labeled a "Stalker"-Stan, perhaps as much as women fear being labeled "Easy"-Esther.

You might be thinking, "But a godly man should pray for wisdom from the Holy Spirit to guide his motivation of whom to pursue. If he heeds this wisdom I shouldn't have to do anything to catch his eye." I've heard this argument from many women. While it does have perfect Christian merit, I ask you a question in return. If a homeless old man, smelly, in tattered clothes, nearly toothless, and with open sores said to you, "The Holy Spirit told me you were the one I should pursue," would you accept a date with him? I don't think you would. So let's put to rest the notion that you would obey the Holy Spirit in such cases or even in more realistic cases when a godly man for whom you simply feel no attraction asks you out.

What we are left with is a man's sense of attraction to guide his pursuit behavior. There's no going to the Lord for

permission to feel that attraction for a woman; it just happens. Why wouldn't a Christian woman consider a man's
sense of attraction to her a natural and healthy consequence
of the way God created men? My guess is that Christian
women unnecessarily make simple attraction into a complicated spiritual issue. Maybe that skewed perspective is a consequence of all the Mr. Wrongs who broke her heart. After all,
in her inexperience, she entered into those risky relationships
based on raw attraction.

Moreover, a woman's suggestion to a man to pray for wisdom first before asking her out may just be her way of feeling
permission from God to say yes to the man's future date invitation. In most cases she will never truly know if he prayed
first. Hence, her prayer criterion turns out to be a lesson in
self-hypnosis, brainwashing, self-deceit...whatever. Her
desired end result is that she feels justified in accepting a date
with him. In addition she feels more comfortable or protected
by God to let herself be the wonderfully vulnerable woman
(stifling her overly fierce sense of independence) that she longs
to be with Mr. Right. It is unsettling to me that a Christian
woman requires "permission" from God who is already in
control of the whole man-woman attraction process in the
first place.

Once again, that's the beauty of dropping a hint. Doing so
doesn't necessarily lessen the percentage of undesirable
advances from Mr. Wrong. However, dropping hints gives you
some influence over the men by whom you *do want to be
asked out.* I recently had a discussion on this issue with a seventy-seven-year-old man, a retired scientist. Prior to our discussion he, for 20 years, had been in an encore second-wind
volunteer career in criminal justice reform. He made three
good points. First, the Christian man is the leader of the home
in several respects including spiritual, financial, physical, and
educational. The woman, however, is the emotional leader.
This role includes a spirit of accommodation. Second, women
make being pursued by a man a greater challenge than it
should be when they stick together in circles of several
women. "A man has to consider public humiliation if he
breaks into such a circle only to be rejected." Third, when a

man forces himself sexually on a woman without her consent the law calls that rape.

There is a subtle parallel when a man asks out a woman who does not first drop him a hint. In a sense he asks her without her consent. To summarize the seventy-seven-year-old's wisdom, a woman makes herself emotionally accommodating by stepping outside of the spinster's circle and dropping hints, giving a man of her choosing her consent and permission for him to step inside her "space" to ask her out. Both Christian men and women probably don't believe its rape when a man asks out a woman without her "permission". Neither do I. Nevertheless, educated men in the new millennium are hypersensitive about making a woman feel uncomfortable, hence, the increasing reliance on a woman's hint of interest before he will step up to asking her out.

WHY AREN'T WOMEN MARRYING RIGHT OUT OF HIGH SCHOOL?

This is a no-brainer; women want to get their college education. After all, how are they going to take advantage of their equal opportunities in the workforce if they don't have a college degree? Besides, having a college education pays dividends that are more than just financial. College education leads to a greater awareness of the workings of the world around you and the people in it. One learns that there is a certain right to information upon which important life decisions are made. In essence college is a good thing for everyone. I fully promote formal education for all. But why must we put off marriage to get a college degree? Why not get married right out of high school or get married while in college? Well, if parents are doing their job, they somehow convey to their children that they must first get to know their personality, values, ambitions, and lifestyle apart from their parents. This learning period occurs most efficiently when the son or daughter moves out of the parents' home.

189

For those of us who spend our self-honeymoon period of growth in college, we earn a college degree while we learn about ourselves. Once we graduate, if we are not yet married, we naturally look for a job to pay the bills. Also, maybe our exposure to college sparked a specific career path. Last of all, we need to pay back student loans. So it's off to work we go.

Knowing that a job is inevitable after college we start to wonder how finding Mr./Miss Right will fit our plan. Will my girlfriend relocate with me if I take this job? Will she be able to get a job in her field if she does? The long and short of it is that newly college educated singles will subconsciously assess the probability that they will find a future spouse in college who will also find a suitable job in the same town. To add to this unlikelihood both will have to consider moving away from their family/hometown. Hence, to avoid the improbable you go where you can get a job and decide that you will find a mate in that town. Well, work isn't as populated with people about your age like college was, so now the odds of finding a suitable mate are immediately reduced.

What societal changes have increased the delay factor for getting married out of high school? Is it that women today go to college and embark on a career before thinking about marriage? Is it because men have gotten used to the idea that women want to first pursue a career after college graduation? Have women lost their role for dropping hints?

I speculate that it is not the increased opportunities for women that are causing this delay factor. Why shouldn't women get degrees and careers regardless of whether or not men are pursuing them? After all single women must afford their lifestyle while they hope for Mr. Musing to come along. In short, women want to be self-sufficient. And perhaps based on what women witnessed in their parents' marriage, new college women graduates who are single don't want to jump hastily into a marriage that statistically only has about 50 percent chance of not ending in divorce like her parent's marriage did. Young singles take a vow not to get married until they figure out what's right for them and can afford to enjoy what's right for them so as not to make the same mistake their parents made. Besides, what's the hurry?

To conclude, the entity that knocks on your door is a combination of two forces. One part is the Big Bad Wolf of popular culture and media that wants to make money off you. The second is your own conscience jam packed full of memories, experiences and, if you're blessed, advice from your elders. Both of these sources of influence will be incessant door-knockers placing a spell on your mind. Hopefully you will be able to filter out the negative influence and focus on the influence of the Holy Spirit in making your life-decisions. In the context of this book the best way to break any spell, of course, is to drop subtle hints.

CHAPTER 14

STEP INSIDE THE MAN-HUDDLE

A Man's Fantasy

(Fade in the carefully selected mood music)

Okay! I'll stop right here. *Bvvvvveeeeertttt*! (That's the sound of an old-fashioned stereo diamond stylus sliding across a vinyl album . . . ask your parents). There's no way that as a Christian author I'm going to get away with illustrating a man's fantasy. But I must broach the topic of pornography nonetheless. First let me describe a man's fantasy in the context of reality. All he really wants from you is a hint that you are interested in his attention. He will respond to your hint by approaching you and making charming conversation. His fantasy is made perfect if when he asks you out for coffee or for your e-mail address you simply say *yes* with a delighted look on your face. That's it. Got it? Good. Now back to the porn issue.

The main observation that inspired this book is that women seem to have lost the fine art of dropping hints. No, not all men but just the ones she likes. Having lost that art, men have little reason for mingling with women other than for someone to talk to while they wait for Miss Right to arrive and drop a hint.

Once again I ask you, how does that expression rub you? "Women seem to have lost the fine art of dropping hints." I need to revisit this question periodically to determine if your mind has changed (or not) since answering that question earlier in this book. Do you feel that the expression is suggesting that in order to find a husband you have to demean yourself at the foot of a man? I can see how a woman with destructive pride might take it that way. Try thinking about it this way. Although dropping something at the foot of a man doesn't conjure up illusions of romance, doing so demonstrates the giving of a *gift* to a man.

My prayer in writing this book is that you come to view your role as a single Christian woman as that of dropping the precious gift of a subtle hint. Speaking as a man, this gesture is a gift beyond measure. In a previous block (Chapter 5: HUMAN EQUIVALENT OF PHEROMONES: THE HINTS) I do my best to identify such hints so that you can add them to your repertoire of male head-turning tactics. Suffice it to say for now that I'm not asking you to throw yourself at his feet or fawn; just be imaginative, subtly direct, and persistent. I believe you will be surprised at how little effort you must make to be successful at it. The hardest part will involve stifling your destructive pride and allowing yourself to be vulnerable in the process of hint dropping, not to mention dodging the acrid stares and comments from other women. "She looks so foolish; she must be *really* desperate."

Because single Christian women have lost the art of dropping subtle hints there is little dating activity going on in Christian singles group. Now enter the dragon. I can speculate on another reason why this trend is so. It has nothing to do with the women; it's actually the men who have lost something. Men may have lost the libido that drives them toward romantic relationships with women. And the dragon responsible for this reduced libido is pornography. I am really speculating now, because I have not personally read a published study that surveyed Christian men for their use of pornography. I have heard preachers refer to such studies so I assume they're legitimate statistics (as a brief aside the same preachers report that women also suffer from the same temptation although not nearly as significantly as men). Suffice it to say that most Christian men struggle with the temptation of pornography, myself included.

Given easy access to porn online, in local video stores, in newsstands, yes even on billboards, women's magazines, TV shows, TV commercials, department store catalogues, and on and on, it doesn't take a stretch of the imagination to conclude that many men fall prey to that dragon in its many forms both public and private. In a previous section (Chapter 3: HEAR ME ROAR) I spell out a number of things that a man has to compete with in order to measure up to a woman's expectation, including her father's social standing and economic power. Likewise a woman is competing for a man's loyalty to his mother for all the nurturing and tender loving care she has provided before he met you. Let's face it. A man's mom is a heavyweight contender to you. Pornography is a close second contender.

Men who use porn habitually will develop an unrealistic mental template of a woman that satisfies his sexual desires. When he meets women at the Christian singles group, he takes a quick mental snapshot of her physical presence and compares it to his mental template. Given the physical criteria of porn stars, chances are that she is not going to measure up to his mental template. He's probably glad to meet her, but she may have to poke him in the eye to see if he is really paying any attention to her. Believe me when I say that a good poke in his eye is when a woman drops him a hint. It's as if he's spellbound until she snaps her fingers in his face (her subtle hint) to break him out of his porn-induced indifference.

A Lecture to Men

We men know that pornography is an offense against God and women. But it gives single men a visual stimulus for sexual arousal and the awesome God-created gift of orgasm. We also know that ultimately orgasm was created to be enjoyed in the context of marriage. We single men know we are sinners and find it almost impossible to measure up to God's standards for sex. Each of us men has to face daily how we fail to meet that standard. The biblical issues surrounding the use of porn for masturbation (male and female) will not be further examined in this book. A representative from your local Christian church, however, can arrange to meet with you for further dialogue on this issue.

The focus of this lecture will be on the impact of porn on a man's motivation to pursue Miss Right when he meets her. As a man are you part responsible for the lack of pursuit behavior in your singles group because of the comfort and solace you find in viewing porn? When you are physically attracted to a woman in your singles group do you shy away from pursuing her for fear of rejection? Do you favor porn because there is no fear of rejection? If you stopped watching porn don't you think your pursuit for women would become less passive and more active and intentional? There's a reason why eunuchs in biblical times were entrusted to guard women in the privacy of their homes; eunuchs have no male genitalia. Does your use of porn render you like a eunuch, devoid of an incentive to pursue women?

If you feel that your pursuit behavior for women is compromised by the influence of porn I recommend that you remove yourself from singles group meetings and functions. It's not because you are struggling with that issue but because you are not adding to the interactive verve of the room. In a previous section (Chapter 10: Who Belongs in a Christian Singles Group?) I suggest that women with issues that compromise *their* hint-dropping motivation also not attend the singles group for the same reason. For both men and women there is much forgiveness for our issues. As part of a forgiving community we should not hold others sins against them. We all confess and repent on our own time and conviction. Meanwhile if you cannot contribute to the interactive dating verve of your singles group its best if you don't attend.

Mister Brave Doesn't Exist But Master Brave Did...Once

Men experiment with being Mr. Brave early on in childhood, but cumulative bouts with rejection taint his innocent and naive perspective. What follows are examples from my childhood where I played Mr. Brave. As you read think about how similar past events among the single men in your social circle might impact their pursuit motivation towards you.

SALLY

I was old enough to ride my bike for a year or two. I don't have kids now, so I don't know what age that was. My next-door neighbor, Sally, was just learning to ride hers. I was not very interested in playing with her because, after all, she was a dull, fragile girl; I was a very active boy. It wasn't too sur-prising, though, that our two playgroups crossed paths every so often. I have two younger sisters and they had friends; we occasionally all interacted. Sally and I ended up riding our bikes with each other in a circle on the quiet street in front of our two houses. We didn't talk much, but both of us concen-trated on keeping in a circle formation as we rode. I don't know about her, but I felt a communion with her.

After we rode for a few minutes, we stopped because of dizziness or sheer boredom. In a moment or two I asked her, "Will you be my girlfriend?"

She said, "Okay."

And we rode in circles some more. We were both delighted.

What seemed to be a few days later, her family moved away and I never saw her again. More likely I just got bored of the idea and went back to my boy-group. She really did move away soon after our bike ride.

LAURA

In kindergarten I met Laura. She lived, on the other side of the three-foot wide creek running through a small parkland between our neighborhoods. She was cute and I liked her. I don't know how it happened but we ended up meeting at the creek after school. We talked for a few minutes, and I asked her to marry me.

She said, "Okay."

I invited her that moment to come back to my house to meet my mom. After a five-minute walk to the back door of my house, I said to Laura, "Wait here while I go get my mom."

"Okay."

"Mom! Mom! There's someone I want you to meet at the back door. We're going to get married."

"Oh! Isn't that wonderful! Okay, just a second while I take off my apron."

"Are you coming, Mom?"

"Yes, here I come. What's her name so I know how to greet her?"

"Laura."

We both walked out the back door, and Laura was nowhere to be found.

"She was here when I came in. She must have gone home."

"Maybe she will come by later."

"Yes. She must have to go home for dinner or something."

"Yes, I think so."

I ran back to the place in the creek where we met, but there was no sign of her. I don't remember seeing her again, but she didn't move away. Maybe I simply moved on and forgot about her, but didn't forget the experience. We met again in high school but we were clearly running in two very different crowds.

Dona

In sixth grade I sat across the aisle from Dona in math class but couldn't think of anything to say to her. One day I turned to her and quietly called her name. She looked over and I contorted my face with my fingers to try and get her to laugh.

From the front of the classroom I heard the teacher call out, "Mr. Beck, you find it funny to disrupt my class? Why don't you come to the front of the class and show everyone your new look?" So I went up there and presented my new face to the class. I don't remember if anyone laughed. I felt silly. But worse I felt defeated that my face didn't make Dona laugh. Then it was fifteen minutes of standing in the back corner of the classroom.

Later that same year was my school's annual musical for the parents. Each grade level would pull all its students and sing and dance for about ten minutes in the social hall. The students would remain in their classrooms before and after their performance until all the performances were finished. It was a two-hour event. I was still smitten with Dona. While we waited our turn to perform, someone started passing around a T-shirt with a marker for everyone to sign. The shirt came to me before it got to Dona. So I passed it by without signing it. After everyone else signed it the shirt was returned to the owner. I got up out of my seat and went over to the owner and said, "I didn't get to sign it yet. Can I take it back to my desk for a moment?" With the marker in my hand I signed my name below Dona's putting a plus sign between our names and drew a love heart encircling our two names. This move got back to Dona in a matter of minutes. When she found out she immediately got the shirt and with the marker slashed out my name and the heart around our names. She was indignant; I was humiliated and heartbroken.

A RECENT MARRIAGE PROPOSAL

Just recently I was at my local public recreation area installing a permanent boundary line on the sand volleyball court. The kids' playground and jungle gym was within earshot about twenty yards away. It was getting dark fast, so I was in a bit of a rush all the while eavesdropping on their uninhibited banter. There were about six kids there.

In short order I noticed one boy was mainly focusing his boy-behavior in the direction of this one girl, probably a year or two younger than he. Out of nowhere he interjected, "Will you marry me?" And before he could take his next breath she replied loud and empathically, "No!"

Then I paid a little more attention to see what the aftermath would be like for them. To my amazement they immediately returned to their previous repartee with each other. No harm, no foul; no signs of hurt feelings in the boy, no signs of anticipation in the girl that he would bother her by asking her again. In fact a few minutes later three of these kids including the boy and girl came over and onto the volleyball court to inquire about what I was doing. I usually enjoy moments like that to make a mental connection with kids but not this time.

It was getting dark, the parents were nowhere to be seen, and I didn't want any attention drawn to what I was doing with the boundary line. (I didn't get permission from the county park to install it.) So I said, "I'm installing this boundary line for the volleyball court. Say, would you kids mind going back over to the jungle gym while I finish up here? It's getting dark and I have to hurry to get this done." They got their answer and just as quickly ran off to the jungle gym to continue their play.

I am from a large family of equal boys and girls. As children we dealt with each other instantly with our mouths and if necessary with physical "coercion". There was no such thing as politically correct phraseology. We said whatever was in our spontaneous inclination. It was conflict resolution in its most primitive yet efficient form. What does Scripture say about conflict resolution? Get it done before sundown, right? As kids we got it done before the next breath, and it was forgotten by sundown. In my twenties I often wondered why adults couldn't do it the same way.

I remember bemoaning one reality check that as adults, conflict resolution cannot be carried out in the word choice and physical reactivity of children. It was a sad reality check for me and quite frankly some twenty years later my first inclination is to react spontaneously with no check on my phraseology. Hence, I am prone to saying something hurtful even if what I say is intended to ultimately be helpful, this book being a prime example. But when I do catch myself and button my lip closed I end up saying nothing (when a politically correct response is in order) which makes me a non-communicator. I don't like that about my personality, and it often times causes unnecessary strain on my work, church, and family relationships. Interestingly, however, more than one of my past girlfriends has said that I have no problem with communication in the relationship. I'm not sure why it doesn't carry over into all areas of my life but it just doesn't.

Anyway, the banter and the marriage proposal that I witnessed next to the jungle gym was refreshing to my soul, even though my adult reality is a bit more complex. Sadly, though, I know that this wonderfully honest and spontaneous type of communication is still within me and probably in every other adult male on this planet as well. I believe all men would be much more fearless in their approach to communicating with women and much more fearless with a date proposal if only women would relearn how to drop subtle hints. And just like the jungle-gym girl, if you answer "no" to a date invitation, it should not become the source of public information. Continue conversing with him as if nothing awkward happened. And remember, what happens at the jungle gym stays at the jungle gym.

MEN'S DESTRUCTIVE PRIDE

On top of adolescent scars add another element that seems to come a few years after puberty. Once again, I call it destructive pride to distinguish it from healthy productive pride. That element is protection of one's ego from the feelings of shame and embarrassment associated with rejection.

The reality is that if you are attending a Christian singles group and a man approaches you, he is already likely to be in the destructive pride-preservation mode. That is to say that men will be in a mode that serves to minimize past behavior (i.e., being Mr. Brave) that led to the unpleasant experience (rejection, laughs behind his back, gossip). He is about to defy everything in his past, in his memory, and in his better judgment that reminds him of the personal pride risk of approaching you.

Clearly this type of pride is of the destructive variety. Nevertheless he approaches you mostly because of the alternative consequences of remaining single for the rest of his life and also because of the incredible physical attraction he feels for you. Now you have his vulnerability in the palm of your hand. What decision will you make? How will you deliver that decision? Women owe men nothing less than their honesty and appreciation for an offer despite a yes or no decision. *Nothing less!*

Do you now see that a man's past experiences, even back as far as childhood, may factor into his pursuit behavior? He has a subconscious need for some kind of sign from you that he has some chance of receiving a "yes" in response to his invitation. As a child it was acceptable to be spontaneous and unfettered. But as an adult there are complex social guidelines of verbal communication including being sensitive about who to engage socially. In conclusion I hope my anecdotes help you to understand the vital importance in your role and the impact on men of dropping hints.

Ready.........BREAK! (a signal from the quarterback to the other players in the huddle to break out and execute the planned action)

CHAPTER 15

STEP INSIDE THE WOMAN-CIRCLE

THE WAITING GAME

"I waited patiently for the LORD; he inclined to me and heard my cry."
(Psalms 40:1, *The Holy Bible*. English Standard Version.)

That verse of Scripture is used in various Christian worship songs and seems to be the mantra of many singles waiting for the Lord to provide Mr./Miss Musing. There is a picture I found online that goes hand-in-hand with that mantra. I could not believe my eyes when I stumbled upon it. In fact I used that image as my manuscript cover when I was asking people to read it for feedback, pre-publication. Please, please, PLEASE stop reading now and do a Google search to look at the image. The link is below. In case the link doesn't work (worked fine at manuscript submission) the title is "Awaiting Christ's Return". In brief the picture includes a woman sitting on a white porch swing under a tree branch. She is dressed in a white flowing gown. Next to her on the swing is a pillow with the words "Awaiting Christ's Return" embroidered on it. The backdrop is the image of a larger than life Jesus holding a basket of bread with his gaze directed to her. The woman in the picture projects a forlorn expression on her face not looking at Jesus but looking forward at the viewer. My take on the picture is that she is hopeful yet passive in her wait for Mr. Musing. In the meantime she'll wait on the Lord.

View number 53 at:
http://s269.photobucket.com/albums/jj77/godsrose123/?action=view&current=WaitingforChristreturn.gif&mediafilter=images

Indeed, it appears that women are of the attitude that if they wait in their home on the back swing or in their apartment long enough, then God will send the perfect mate to knock on their door. This provision would indeed be a blessing of the Lord.

It wasn't long after attending my first Christian singles group that I concluded the following.

"The women in attendance here don't appear to be dropping hints of interest to any men. They must be waiting for Jesus Christ Himself to return for a date..." I pointed this observation out to one woman and added, *"...but Jesus is already married to the Church! So you better lower your standards a little."*

I interpret the image of Jesus looking over her in two ways. Firstly, she is overly preoccupied with Jesus' care and attention making her *not of this world*. Secondly, her preoccupation with Jesus becomes her mental template upon which Mr. Right will have to measure.

Do waiting tactics work for you? While you wait sitting in your apartment, did the Lord bring a prospective employer with a job to your door? Did your current landlord deliver a videotape of your current apartment and lease contract to your door for you to sign? Does the local grocery store manager deliver the food you need for sustenance to your door? Did the local car dealership drive your current car to your door to sell it to you? When you need money from your bank account, does the banker show up with a handful of cash? When you were church shopping, did you invite pastors to your apartment to listen to their doctrinal "pitch"?

The obvious answer to all these hypothetical questions is *no* unless you pay someone for that service. The point is that there are many examples in your daily routine where you rely on the blessing of your Christian judgment and initiative to make God-glorifying decisions.

Making God-glorifying decisions and dealing with all those hypothetical questions in the above paragraph is an active process in which you must step up to the decision plate, exert some effort, and use discernment. Why should finding a mate be any different? Yet you might say, "But I do go out to singles groups and participate in the social events, and I do have conversations with men."

But let me ask you, are you dropping hints? If not, you might just as well be home in your apartment behind a closed door. When you are not dropping hints, you remove yourself from men's subconscious radar-detector akin to hiding yourself away behind your apartment front door. There's only one way to break through the feeling of apartment isolation and that is by dropping hints.

Singles who believe that a great demonstration of faith is to sit and wait at home on the back swing for God's blessings to occur need a reality check. Waiting in faith on God's provision in the case of many Christian singles is more a statement that they've screwed up in the past on important decisions for their life. They have consequently renounced taking the risk of doing that again, so they put all that decision-making power in the hands of the Lord. On the surface that sounds pretty righteous, right? Wrong!

Well, maybe in some cases. What I conclude is that we don't want to face the consequences of our own decisions anymore, so we will wait for the Lord to make tough decisions for us or put those decisions in the hands of somebody else. In the case of marriage, women put that decision in the hands of a man. Whoa! I'm a man and I don't like the way that sounds. A man can make a decision to pursue a woman, but he cannot make her decide to like him. He does his best to present himself to her, but she ultimately decides yes or no.

The indecisive waiting mentality is the opposite of faith. Furthermore, faith is most obviously manifested and demonstrated when we make God-glorifying decisions. We praise Him for the consequences of the good ones and are humbled by or edified by the ones that turn out to be bad. Even the best accountability partner is human and will not be able to head off all our flawed plans. Faith is required to know that you are forgiven for the bad decisions and that you are willing to accept forgiveness, learn from your decisions, and try again with the new lessons learned of what God has taught you. Avoiding this process leads to stagnation and is a fear-based way of conducting your life.

Finding Mr. Right is no exception to the necessary trial and error process. The good news is that all it takes from women to avoid stagnation in their quest for Mr. Right is to drop hints. Doing so may not seem like you're making a major decision or taking discreet action, but when your hint is dropped at the right man, it will start a steadily building volcanic reaction inside of him. Just step back and watch him erupt into godly action in pursuit of you. Maybe your hint will simply fizzle out in him like a bad fuse. You'll never know which it will be unless you drop a hint.

Oh yes, and what about those secluded women to whom God did send a man to their apartment door for marriage? Well, those women end up marrying plumbers, postmen, Fed Ex/UPS men, milkmen, carpet installers, cable guy, Fuller brush salesman, and home heating oil delivery men. Do you see the commonality amongst these professions? That's right! They all must visit or work at the customer's home. They all end up at your door not motivated by love but motivated by making a dollar from you (one exception would be if Jehovah Witnesses were to show up at your door; they don't want your money but instead your membership).

The motivation of making a buck by these tradesmen does not, however, rule out that the chemistry between you is mutual and authentic. There's no reason why it wouldn't work out. It's just a shame for women who wait at home that male medical doctors no longer make house calls.

Both women *and* men can cop an attitude of hiding by vowing that, "I will go about my normal daily life, not going out of my way to meet Mr./Miss Right. The Lord will put someone in my path when He sees fit for me." And I agree. But tell me. How do you behave on your path? Do you have your eyes glued to a book or otherwise looking down at the sidewalk or iPod connected to your ears? Do you avoid eye contact thinking that Mr./Miss Right will bulldoze through your walls to talk to you/drop you a hint? Some singles have the self-defeating attitude that if they simply walk their normal path they will meet Mr./Miss Right. But the problem is that they tend to find clever ways of hiding within themselves along this path. Who is going to approach a hider? While you walk your walk you must also remember to be receptive and open and approachable to the person that the Lord has set on your daily path.

WOMEN WON'T BUDGE FOR ANYONE SAVE MR. BRAVE

Women seem to have the notion that men have nerves of steel. They seem to believe that a man will (or should) approach them despite having no indication from her regarding whether or not she would say yes to an invitation for a date. I can't help but have the following unrealistic sequence go through my mind. It reflects what I can only guess is some women's fanciful notions of how Mr. Brave will approach her.

A WOMAN'S FANTASY

Mr. Brave steps into the doorway, pausing momentarily before pushing into the crowded room. From across the room you see him. His flowing full head of hair, his chiseled jaw and cheekbones, his composure, his unspoken yet entrancing demeanor...unforgettable. His piercing eyes are locked on yours. Suddenly every other object and person in the room blurs to insignificance; all sound diminishes except the pounding of your heart, the breath through your mouth and surge of warmth throughout your being. Looking neither left nor right, he moves with alluring self-confidence in your direction.

You wishfully conclude that he is probably much too arrogant to be God's gift to you. Nevertheless, your whole body tingles and you blush against your will. You drop the defense from around your guarded heart momentarily, just long enough to imagine that he *is* God's gift to you, humble and completely unaware of his own magnetic charisma. His engaging face is mesmerizing; your lower jaw drops subtlety, and your lips part involuntarily desperate to inhale the breath he has just taken away from you.

After what seems like hours, he finally stands in front of you, eyes still fixed on yours. A spreading smile graces his face now beaming as he extends his hand to *you* in a gesture of introduction. You return the gesture and as your hand slips into his you feel the essence of his warmth envelop your heart.

"Hello, my name is Tom. Is this seat taken?"

You quickly and subtly toe-kick your best friend's purse and Bible away from underneath the empty seat next to you.

"I can't believe that there's an empty chair next to such a beautiful woman."

Bvvvvveeeertttt! And now you're back to reality as your best friend nudges you as she sits down next to you.

She asks sarcastically, "Did Mr. Right try to take this seat while I was gone?"

SORRY, BUT BACK TO REALITY

Uhemm . . . Miss . . . Miss!? Can you come back to the text of my book? Where did your mind go while you read the last section? Did Mr. Musing do it for you? When was the last time Mr. Musing presented himself to you in such a manner? Not in your dreams, but in reality? You're lucky if it happens once every other lifetime.

No, I don't believe in reincarnation; it's an expression to reflect my opinion that guys who present themselves to women like Mr. Musing are so rare that most women will probably never experience him. That is, unless you are a movie actress and then it probably happens pretty often on the set. But that's not reality.

For men a parallel analogy to Mr. Musing would be getting a hint of interest from Miss Beauty Queen. She only exists in movies, Miss America pageants and beauty products TV commercials. But that's not reality either, or at least not *most* men's reality.

PREFERRED APPROACH: UNPREDICTABLE

If indeed the scenario illustrated above in section A WOMAN'S FANTASY is valid, what follows in this section will demonstrate that women can be very unpredictable in their preferences for the manner in which they want to be approached by Mr. Musing. This unpredictability adds more uncertainty to a man's evaluation of a woman that is in addition to the uncertainty of whether or not she is interested or attracted to him in the first place.

I posed the following scenario to Sherri, ironically the same woman who in chapter 3: THE MILLION-DOLLAR QUESTION asked me, "Eddie B., what's wrong with the men in this group? Why aren't they asking anyone out?" In my conversation with her, I painted a scenario in which a man walks up to her after the service and introduces himself. She doesn't know him, but chances are he has seen her before. In fact, unbeknownst to her, he's been summoning up his courage for weeks to introduce himself. Anyway I ask, is it okay or not for a man to walk up to you and simply introduce himself to you? Here's her reply:

> *"I would feel very uncomfortable with that, I mean, he knows nothing about me so what is the basis for his interest in meeting me? Well, I mean, he could simply feel superficial attraction toward me. But there should be more to it than that."*

So I ask you. What's wrong with a guy's motivating factor simply being inspired by superficial attraction? Is that a crime or biblical sin? No! On the contrary, that kind of attraction is made in the image and likeness of God. However, when a guy doesn't follow up with getting to know a woman's character (and vice versa), he is just stupid (and if she doesn't she is too). And there's no way to know if he's stupid or not unless she gives him a chance to prove it. It is equally probable that he'll learn that *she* has no character and will leave her alone. She may not know who he is because he might be a latecomer Mark the Shark (who only shows up at the end of service with seduction on his mind) or more likely the two of them quite simply were not at the same services or same church activities. They've just been missing each other.

If a woman's church is super huge it's understandable that she will not know every man in attendance. Regardless, is she going to reject a potential suitor just because she's never seen him before, or is she going to behave like a mature adult and practice sensible discretion? Does her mother still warn you not to talk to strangers? That was timely advice when she was naive; but now she's an adult. It's time for her to use her God-given capacity of discernment. For all she knows this new guy may be a trusted friend of a cousin or someone similarly close.

I am actually doubtful of alleged Mark the Sharks showing up at the end of a church service to pick up women. If you know for sure that you have one on your hands give him your testimony about how you became a Christian. That should ward him off. That way you glorify God by giving your testimony and you demonstrate an adult approach toward screening out the sharks.

In another section (chapter 11: JUST SAY IT) I discussed the vital importance of Christian women being honest and direct when rejecting men. And if you don't handle rejecting men in this manner, you have probably left some bitter men in your wake. Yet these men are your brothers and should be keeping a watchful eye out for characters such as Mark the Shark. Wouldn't you find it helpful if one of your brothers tapped you on the shoulder and said, "Hey, Lisa, better watch out for that guy Mark. I've spoken with him on several occasions and it's difficult to get a sense of where his heart is."

Although you will ultimately make your own decisions regarding Mark, isn't it, nevertheless, helpful to have this kind of input from your brothers? But get this: as sinful as it is if you go around using deception and avoidance as part of your rejection repertoire, many of your rejected brothers are going to hold back on their warnings of Mark the Shark ultimately resulting in you getting your comeuppance.

To conclude, a woman's preferred approach appears to be as follows. On one hand she wants to be asked out by men preferably without having to drop him a hint. On the other hand she is uncomfortable with being asked out when he is initially attracted to her superficial beauty. On one foot she has romantic notions of Mr. Musing sweeping her off her feet while making her feel emotionally safe. On the other foot the cold-turkey approach from a man she doesn't know makes her feel uncomfortable.

In essence a woman is expecting a man to evaluate each one of those four other "appendages" before he approaches her being absolutely sure he fulfills her criteria. There are two problems with this womanly way of thinking about her Mr. Musing. Firstly, we men are not mind readers so we don't know what your tolerance is for each criterion (i.e. if he is handsome and well-educated it's OK if I don't know him so well). Secondly, each woman's tolerance is different so we men are left with no universal rules to assess the suitability of a cold-turkey pursuit of any one woman. Any nearly statistically insignificant deviation from your peculiar criteria could result in Mr. Musing getting an unfair reputation of being Mr. Mark the Shark, Stalker Stan or worse. Do you see how dropping hints gives us men your unspoken invitation to step up to the date invitation plate?

ENTER BACHELOR CONSOLATION PRIZE

Now that you've accepted that, statistically speaking, you will never experience an approach by Mr. Musing, you might be willing to let that fantasy vanish into thin air. *Poof!* Let it be gone. Thus, you will need to have a backup image of how

Mr. Not-as-Brave (Mr. Consolation Prize) will present himself.

Let me first confess (as if by now it's not painfully obvious) that I am bitter about being single. You've probably already concluded that by page one, but I feel the need to come clean. Yes, I am bitter about my marital status, and I'm constantly pointing my blaming finger at single Christian women. For better or worse, I suppose that bitterness is my motivation for writing this book. I hope this book is informative to Christian woman who are steeped in a chaotic culture of genderless roles in the area of attraction and the opposite sex. You *do* have the God-given gift of attracting Mr. Righteous. I hope by reading this book you will know how to unwrap that gift, letting it arise out of your inordinately guarded, bitter or destructively prideful heart.

I feel better now that I've come clean. Now it's back to the topic of this section. So you've dropped your hint to me, Mr. Consolation Prize (Mr. C). I detect your hint and introduce myself. In a matter of thirty seconds, you sense the appearance of multiple awkward pauses in our nascent conversation. You conclude to yourself, "(Fill in the blank here with whatever you think in this scenario because I don't have a clue)."

I don't know what you conclude, but the look on your face after one too many awkward pauses screams out to me, *"Run away! Run away! He's NOT Mr. Musing; he's NOT Mr. Musing!"* And you do run away. I throw up my hands in frustration and while my arms are up I take a whiff of my armpits to see if I have offensive body odor (which I do not).

What is it about women and awkward pauses in conversations? Are you under the impression that every man is a Martin Luther King, Jr.? I have witnessed many single Christian men who simply have the gift of "gab." I do *not* have that gift; it's just not in my natural timing of conversation. Indeed, there are many, many awkward pauses in my conversations with single women especially during the "get to know" phase. From my observations the men who do well in smoothing through awkward pauses are men who can talk about how green the grass is and make it interesting to you as well. I don't have that talent and admittedly I don't *want* that talent if it means attracting a woman who is captivated by conversation at the level of green grass.

Obviously I don't recommend conversation starters such as "How long was your last relationship and how did it end?" I believe there is a middle ground. To conclude, if you want *substance* from a man, you'll just have to suffer through those awkward pauses until you get to know each other a little better. He might not be Mr. Musing but Mr. C is all you've got. Like good wine Mr. C just takes time to ferment into Mr. Musing. Give him the benefit of time. Don't worry; in the process you don't risk missing out on meeting Mr. Musing (because at best he only shows up once every other life time).

F: What goes through your mind during awkward pauses with Mr. C?

CHAPTER 16

DON'T OPEN THAT CAN-O-WORMS!

DELVING A LITTLE DEEPER

What runs through a woman's mind that causes her unease during awkward moments in conversations? Is she afraid of what a man might be thinking about her? Is she afraid of the intense intimacy that nonverbal eye-to-eye contact elicits? Does she fear revealing an uncontrollable blush in his presence? Do those brief moments instantaneously reveal her completely irrational (but God-blessed) desire to be his wife, mother of his children and his partner in retirement? Is he thinking the same thoughts? Does she recoil from such self-revelations for fear of rejection or even commitment for that matter? What is it in a woman that prevents her from simply basking in such glorious nonverbal moments even when she ironically *is* attracted to the man? Does she rationalize that it's not polite to stare? Is she under the Hollywood impression that men who engage in long awkward stares may be a threat to her physical security?

In some slave cultures and even modern day militaries, eye-to-eye contact is forbidden between "boss and employee" in times when strict control and submission are "critical"! Do you agree that the ability for adults to hold eye-to-eye contact (even during pauses, indeed *especially* during pauses) is *healthy* and not Hollywood threatening? Do you equate the *lack* of awkward pauses with a high degree of common interests? Taking it a step further, do you equate lack of awkward

213

pauses with both short-term attraction and long-term compatibility?

I suspect that women place a very high value on men who can converse without allowing awkward pauses to creep into the dialogue. In fact, let me make an even bolder statement. Women may be so inordinately sensitive to awkward pauses that they often mistake Mr. Glib for Mr. Right. Have you ever opted for a man (Mr. Glib) who can keep a conversation going but with whom you know you have little in common? Moreover, have you ever rejected a man (Mr. Right) who is comfortable with awkward pauses yet who may also be compatible with your long-term marriage feelings and desires? If you continue to opt for Mr. Glib just be prepared to be the one to introduce subjects that are conducive to learning about each other's character. Otherwise you may learn a lot about how the green grass grows. After a few dates of that maybe you won't mind "suffering" through awkward pauses with Mr. Right.

For me, gazing into a woman's eyes is far more awe inspiring than flying over the Grand Canyon, rafting down a class 5 river, watching the single channel currents of an ion channel flicker across a computer screen, leading a worship band in praise of the Lord... Eye-gazing is a reflection to me of how awesome is the Lord God Almighty!

Truth is that men are also reluctant to suffer through awkward pauses in conversations. I know my essence is sinful; that's why I need Jesus' shed blood for redemption. Yet dwelling on my sinful essence would mean *not* living a life free from my sinful essence. How unpleasant that would be to God who sacrificed His Son so that I could live freely, paying attention to the Holy Spirit and glorifying God instead of wallowing in my sinful essence. Thus, when I gaze into a woman's eyes I see beyond the sinful essence and instead I see into the eye of God's best creative work yet. Her name is *Woman.*

Next time you lock eyes with Mr. Right hold your gaze until he looks away first. You might be squirming inside and experiencing a number of physiological responses. Perhaps it is in this moment that your body finally expresses some of those elusive subtle hints. Will you allow its expression or will you squelch it?

Sadly, however, I sense that some women avoid gazing upon men for completely different reasons. I'll explain in the next section, which is pretty hard-hitting.

F: What past experiences in your interaction with men unwittingly determine how long you will hold eye contact during awkward pauses in conversation with him?

UNANSWERED QUESTIONS

Maybe revelation of your essence via awkward pauses is what you fear the most. The Eldredge couple, in their book offers some insight into what a woman might be thinking and feeling during those awkward pauses (Eldredge, John and Stacey Eldredge. *Captivating, Unveiling the Mystery of a Woman's Soul.* Nashville: Thomas Nelson, Inc. 2005)

"Am I lovely?" (p.13,46,59,62)

"Do you see me? Am I captivating? Do I have a beauty all my own?" (p.59,62,108)

She has a "longing to be delighted in, a longing to be beautiful, to be irreplaceable..." (p.46)

She longs "to play an irreplaceable role in a shared adventure." (p.8)

"We (women) are not inviting- we are guarded. Most of our energy is spent trying to hide our true selves, and control our worlds to have some sense of security." (p. 50)

"She becomes a dominating, controlling woman- or a desolate, needy, mousy woman." (p.50)

To women Satan accuses, "You are alone. When they see who you really are, you will be left alone. No one will ever truly come for you." (p.88)

Add to those lies the messages originating from your youth, typically delivered by stressed parents or other frustrated adults around us, "You're worthless, you're not a woman. You're too much. You're not enough. You're a disappointment. You are repulsive." (p.100) All lies, lies, and more lies from Satan to women.

Women are not alone in their attacks from Satan. To men Satan accuses, "Back off (from emotional women), leave her alone. You don't really want to go there. She'll be too much for you." (p.88) Moreover, wounds men suffered as boys often at the hands of their male role models taunt them in adulthood whispering the haunting questions, "Do I have what it takes?", Am I the real deal?", Am I a man?" (p.149)

The Eldredge couple further points out that Satan mainly targets women (as with Eve). Women are "life-givers," reflecting the essence of God, and, therefore, a greater threat to Satan's plan of squelching all life. Women, moreover, are the main driving force for relationship building and maintenance, both one-on-one and in the greater community. Given such satanic attack, it's not surprising that women have much to contend with when it comes to dropping hints and attracting a mate. By the way that book *Captivating, Unveiling the Mystery of a Woman's Soul,* was written for women while *Wild at Heart, Discovering the Secret of a Man's Soul,* Nashville: Thomas Nelson. 2001, was written for men. I highly recommend reading them both from the Eldredge couple.

All of this bombardment certainly takes a toll on a woman's psyche possibly manifesting in feeling awkward in silent pauses during conversation with men. But Satan is tricky. What if you are quite attractive, academically accomplished, hold a high-paying, high-powered position in a highly respected company? You were voted Miss Congeniality in high school and you're nice to even socially awkward people. Satan could be whispering into your ear, "You don't have to drop any hints. Look how beautiful and successful you are. If a man doesn't have the guts to approach you with his confidence, how will he possibly make a good husband and father? Don't condescend to men; you don't need to 'dumb' yourself down for a man. Hold out for the most handsome, eligible bachelor you can. After all, a man won't appreciate you unless he has to vie for you." In this case Satan is playing on your destructive pride. Do you see how repulsive he makes dropping a hint?

I'm finding it difficult to make a concluding statement for this section. All I can come up with is the following: Maintain eye contact, rebuking Satan if need be. Try to focus on the beauty that God has breathed into the man in front of you. Just like women every man has a point of beauty; you just have to be patient enough to let it present itself.

THE CAT ANALOGY

Women are like cats in that a normal healthy cat will warmly greet its owner or a non-threatening guest in the house. Its greeting is often a gentle coiling of its body around your ankles with barely audible purring sounds and pathetic eyes gazing up telepathically saying, "Please give me a good-feeling back scratch!" . Conversely, women are unlikely to peer into a man's eyes and let that request be known. Instead her body language might shout out, "Make me feel better about myself!" And when men, completely unsuspecting of this demand, fail to instantly say something that makes a woman feel better about herself she reflexively runs away. She escapes the man leaving him to ironically wonder, "What did I say?"

IT'S NOT MY JOB

Have you ever seen the iconic picture associated with that slogan? In short a long straight road is shown with a freshly painted double line down the center. Clearly visible is a possum or other small animal laying the middle of the road. Unlike the rest of the road, however, the double yellow lines are painted ACROSS the animal's belly, not on the spot of road below it. Thus, the driver of the double line-painting vehicle did not bother to stop, get out, move the animal and continue painting citing that, "It's not my job (to move animals out of the line of painting)."

Similarly it's not my job or any Christian man's job to instill in Christian women a sense of self-esteem. How did I get to this conclusion? My speculation and answer to the previous section's volley of questions from the Eldredge team is the following. Women who can't hold eye-to-eye contact through the awkward pauses of a conversation are either under Satan's attack or they have low self-esteem issues. Alternatively, she is simply repulsed by the man standing before her in which case she is simply being rude.

It seems that awkward pauses to women are the enemy who mysteriously reveals to the man all her faults, weaknesses, and aspects of her physical body that are not model-perfect—and yet are ironically not even visible due to the clothing or makeup she is wearing (i.e., he can't possibly even know of her imperfections).

Yes, yes, I know you are pretty enraged right now, probably screaming out, "How can this author be so ignorant of the past twenty years that have taught us that woman are truly insecure of their bodies due to mass media exploitation of skinny, blemish-free beautiful women?"

Truth is that I *am* acutely aware of the impact it has on women. I just don't believe it's a brother's, dad's, man's, boyfriend's, fiancé's or husband's role to make amends for such exploitation and the impact it has on women's self-esteem. After all such beautiful women are exploited because they appeal to men, not because they reduce women's self-esteem. For men to apologize for being drawn to such beautiful women would be to berate God for making womem so irresistible.

Self-esteem is not something anyone or anything can give to another; it must be *earned* much like we must earn a good public reputation. You can browse your local bookstore for self-help books geared toward building self-esteem. Moreover professional counseling is available. But to be painfully clear, men are neither counselors nor self-esteem builders. God and *you*, respectively, fulfill those two roles.

I hope you sense a difference between a man who is an encourager and nurturer versus a man who is simply expected to build a woman's self-esteem. A man who perpetually tries to build or maintain a woman's self-esteem is like a Peace Corp volunteer who is constantly handing out bottled water in a third-world country. It would be far better to break the inhabitant's dependence on bottled water by teaching them how to dig a well. I want to be a husband who encourages and nurtures my future wife in such a way that she is *inspired* to face the personal issues (AKA baggage) keeping her from *earning* self-esteem.

Now you know what is *not* a man's job, but then what exactly *is* a man's job in a relationship? His job is to cultivate a sense of commitment to security for his wife. No, not a secure roof or secure brake shoes on the car or secure retirement plan. While these physical securities are also his role, here I refer to emotional, mental, and spiritual security. It is a man's role to demonstrate in words and deeds his committed love for his wife. His role is to preserve and tend to the marriage so that the memory of wedding day vows and honeymoon nights are indeed blissfully taken for granted moment by moment by his wife.

In Hollywood movies male actors make it all look pretty easy; in fact, they make it look uncontrollably natural. Truth is, it's work for the man. How the wife responds to her husband is *her* choice. Furthermore, how she responds will make the man's role blissful or burdensome. Dragging your self-esteem issues into a marriage with hopes that he will fix them is a prescription for marriage misery.

So ask yourself, "Do I exude the essence of self-esteem that will attract a man who will provide me with the security I need to be fully woman around him?" It's not my fault that men can sense a woman's self-esteem through eye-to-eye contact. I can tell you, however, that a woman can fake self-esteem through eye-to-eye contact. *Hmm?* You either have it or not, right? Correct, and no one will know if you're faking or not.

In the counseling profession I believe it's called "role playing." To get counselees to go through the motions of confronting their issues, the counselor will have them act out in healthy ways how they will behave or what they will do in a real-life situation. From a behavioral-physiological point of view (my favorite), such role-playing pioneers a path in the nervous system circuitry that makes subsequent efforts (in real life) a little more spontaneous, less planned, less feared.

To me this whole discussion on eye-to-eye contact and self-esteem is mind-bending. If you test my theory (by role playing) and make eye-to-eye contact with a man and hold it suitably through awkward moments of conversation, he will sense a healthy level of self-esteem. Whether you actually have healthy self-esteem or not is beside the point. From that experience you will want more moments of such eye-to-eye contact with more men and even your friends and family. It can become a sort of addiction that you can "pull it off." Soon enough such eye-to-eye contact becomes effortless and even reflexive, and you find that your self-esteem is soaring. You begin to conduct your life making proactive decisions consistent with your newfound self-esteem and your subconscious body language exudes its fruits.

I don't know what ultimately kicks in the soaring self-esteem. Could it be possible that you've always had it, just never tapped into it? Could it be that our pop culture is the one who convinces women that they don't have self-esteem in the first place? Pop culture may dictate that women lack self-esteem because they were abused, bullied, pushed too hard, raised too strictly, rejected too many times, dated too many Mr. Wrongs. . . What is it about eye contact that reverses this pop cultural miss-indoctrination? I don't know. Is it because eye contact, even through awkward pauses, creates openings for meaningful conversation with your friends and loved ones? Will you also pine for *all* your conversations to be meaningful, even those with Mr. Maybe?

In conclusion (for both men and women) make eye contact, suffer through moments of awkward pauses and refrain from smoothing over such moments with observations on the green grass. Instead permit your quietly engaged presence in front of each other to simply *be* with each other, nothing added but the Holy Spirit.

CHAPTER 17

IT TAKES A VILLAGE...

WHAT ELSE CAN CHURCH LEADERSHIP DO TO HELP ITS SINGLES?

As I mentioned in my INTRODUCTION I can't help but have the feeling that the church leadership gives a sigh of relief after they hire a singles pastor (usually married) and officially sponsor singles gatherings on church campus. Yes, just throw some money at the plight of the singles and hopefully they will eventually marry. Clearly that is not enough; as pointed out by this book the hang-ups between single Christian men and women are far too complex. What follows are suggestions that churches can try in order to get their singles matched up and married. Smart churches will see the practicality in terms of long-term church survival of becoming modern day Yentas for their singles. In other words, having singles marry in their church means children later, hence, members to sustain the future of the church. With a church singles attendance of roughly fifty percent this issue should be equal priority with ministering to traditional families.

Your pastor might argue that the Christian church is not in the business of matchmaking. For reasons mentioned in the above paragraph I obviously disagree. If you suspect that your pastor thinks that way ask him, "If not through church and church sponsored singles activities what better venue can you recommend for me to meet my future spouse? A local bar or nightclub? Civic association meetings? Professional interest meetings?" While each of these venues could surely be a place where you meet your future spouse are they *optimal* venues for finding a future spouse? Are the chances greater at those venues for finding someone equally yoked in the Lord? I doubt it. The local Christian church is *thee* optimal place.

Why would pastors argue against that? That's easy. They don't want to take any responsibility for a divorce should two people that they introduce and marry decide to call it quits after only a few years of marriage. With the divorce rate close to 50% both in and out of the Christian church pastors realize that they don't want to have any onus in the matter. This kind of hand washing by pastors reeks of a lack of faith that God, the Holy Spirit, is present in the pastor's church. Moreover, it is a lack of faith in any premarital or post marital programs that the church might sponsor for its members. Hence, a church can easily explain away its high divorce rate by saying, "We cannot control or influence with whom two people will fall in love. It's a matter of personal conviction that cannot be influenced even if we tried. We can only advise and counsel but in the end the success of the marriage is placed solely on the married couple, not the church." How faithless...how cowardly...how completely lacking in the bigger picture of ministering to singles and future attendance. Genesis 1:28 says, "Be fruitful and multiply and fill the earth and subdue it..." Why *wouldn't* a pastor help his members fulfill God's plan accordingly?

THE BIGGER THE GROUP THE LESS THE SUCCESS

I very much enjoy singles groups with huge attendance numbers. To me it means that the odds are greater that I will find a compatible mate within it. Right? Probably. But I suffer a huge mental block in such situations. I seem to regress into automatic pilot.

Let me explain. My senses in a large room of singles will seek out, mostly visually, the most attractive women. They are the ones that I want to pursue. All other women simply fade into the background. If this is true of other men as well, then

223

we men will all be vying for the same top 5 percent of the woman present.

Of course we will only be vying in our minds because that 5 percent of the women, the Untouchables, are so attractive that they probably don't condescend to the proper role of dropping subtle hints; they are used to guys approaching them cold-turkey.

The long and short of it is that 100 percent of the men are watching 5 percent of the women and they will not notice any other women until those 5 percent Untouchables have been taken or leave the group. Once they leave the next most beautiful 5 percent will become men's focus.

Here's a solution. Get the social committee of your singles group to organize small dinner parties or other interactive events that include no more than five men and five women. This way the men are not distracted by a large pool of women from whom to choose (or at whom to gaze). Their attention can be focused on the five women present and the level of meaningful conversation in the room increases. Married couples can assist in these dinner parties by hosting them in their homes. It's much easier for a man to experience an average woman's personality and warmth when there are fewer women around.

Perhaps that's why the "girl next door" is so beautiful; she's not surrounded by other women (except her mom).

MY WIFE AND I JUST ADOPTED A THIRTY-YEAR OLD

Here's what married couples in your local church can do for the singles of their church. Married families can adopt a single person, or maybe more than one, to get to know them and help pair them up with a compatible mate. Imagine if after the church service singles hung around with their sponsor family instead of bunching up in their gender groups. More meaningful and productive interactions between the sexes can occur when mingling with your host family. Moreover, the married hosts can talk about you in their small group meeting during the week. Such a conversation might go something like the following. "Hi Tom and Jane Smith. You know I saw you talking after service this past weekend with Miss Single that you sponsor. What's she like? What are her hobbies and career/career ambitions, etc.? Oh, really? I think Harold and Martha Jones sponsor Mr. Single that might be a match for her. I'll send the Jones your way after service next weekend."

I believe such behind the scenes help is call social networking the old-fashioned way. The antiquated line from generations past was, "Nice to meet you. Who do you know that I know?" It was as if you had to have a social connection or else it was inappropriate or unsafe to pursue romance.

ANONYMOUS DINNER PARTIES

The married couple sponsors could host dinners where Mr. and Miss Single can meet. It probably works best if the two singles don't know whom each other is. In exchange for hosting the dinner, the married couple can then head out on a date, leaving the two singles behind to clean up and/or babysit. Obviously the married sponsors know their adopted single persons well enough to trust them in their home and/or with their children.

This type of arrangement does two important things. First, it gets one man and one woman away from the sterile group dynamics of the Christian singles group. They can focus on getting to know each other with out the distraction of many alternative people to talk to. Second, the two singles can observe each other in the real-life context of dealing with children and socializing with the marrieds.

I've heard it said enough times by married men that they marvel in watching their wives nurture their children. That male tendency probably doesn't start once they are married with children. So women can take advantage of this effect on men while in the presence of other people's children. The goal is to get yourselves away from the Christian singles group and into a life setting that is much more pertinent to marriage reality.

There's a hidden benefit to dating in such realistic settings. Your rating on the attraction scale becomes less relevant. Not completely irrelevant, just less relevant. Let's muse for a moment. Say you arrange to have dinner with the Smiths and their six children between the ages of one and ten years old. You arrive fashionably late and discover right off that your mystery reality date is Mr. Awkward. Your heart of fanciful expectations drops to your stomach with disappointment. You've had brief conversations with him previously and there just isn't any chemistry whatsoever. You would rate him a 4.5 on the attractiveness scale while you rate yourself 7. Over the course of the night including dinner, cleaning up, and babysitting with this family, you discover that Mr. Awkward magically draws out the untapped creative side of the children's minds. You can only sit back and witness his gift in action. While you are truly amazed you keep asking yourself the same question over and over again, "How did I not see this gift in him before tonight?"

Now imagine that you and I (not your mystery date) previously agreed to meet at the end of the night at home in your apartment for a follow-up interview. My first question would be, now that you have spent some reality time with Mr. Awkward, does your attractiveness rating of him change any? You previously rated him at 4.5. How about now?

My guess is that you would instantly begin to describe the magic that you witnessed Mr. Awkward "perform" with the kids. A revised attractiveness rating is probably not in your vocabulary at the moment. You would end your reply with something like, "I really wasn't expecting Mr. Awkward to come alive like that."

And you would then look at me blankly as if you had thoroughly answered my question. Ahem...just to remind you, the reader, that the question to her was, did your attractiveness rating of him change? Do you see how your emphasis on the "chemistry" shifts to the "reality" of the person? If I pressed you at that moment for a rating number I believe you would be upset with me that I should minimize your experience of Mr. Awkward in favor of a cold, hard number that rates his superficial beauty. You might peevishly say, "Didn't you just hear what I said about this guy?"

What's the take-home message? In small group reality settings you have an opportunity to observe a person from a different perspective. In such settings you have a greater chance of viewing and being viewed for your personality and character. In contrast, at your Christian singles group meetings, the emphasis is on chemistry typified by the attractiveness rating scale. As such, if you want to make that rating scale less significant in your mate selection process, you've got to increase your opportunities for smaller one-on-one-type events.

Incidentally, in the above reality date with the Smith family, the situation could just have well been that *you* at 4.5 were the one to draw out the children's creative side while Mr. Untouchable sat back and watched in amazement.

GET TO KNOW ME DATES: ADVOCACY DATING

As a service to the singles of the church, either the singles group or the church itself can arrange meetings between paired men and women. These "get to know me" dates are purposefully short, say one hour at most. For example, Michael and Michelle are randomly paired for the purpose of getting together for conversation. They are not paired up as potential marriage partners because that would bring too many expectations into the meeting. Instead Michael and Michelle are paired up to be partners in the business of getting their friends "matched-up."

This focus on working together as modern day Yentas is to remove the expectation that they themselves will be "the one" for each other. Thus, Michael and Michelle become advocates for their friends, as if arranging the seating at a wedding reception hoping Michael's friend Dan will enjoy talking and eating next to Michelle's friend Sue. In the process of arranging their friends to meet, Michael and Michelle may discover some romantic feelings for each other. Maybe not. It doesn't matter because they will be working together for the benefit of their friends. And working together for the good of others can be very mutually attractive to the workers.

Alternatively, for singles in their thirties and older, the get-to-know-me dates can be for the determination of their own marriage compatibility. Many Christian singles, despite being 30 and older, may not be used to such marriage-minded dating. To reduce a preponderance of awkward pauses on the date I recommend establishing structured discussion questions.

I know. You're probably asking, "What? Is this a marriage interview?" Well, yes it is! I cannot put out of your mind (or mine) the image of two people showing up in their best business attire with resume in hand and rehearsed answers to typical questions asked at a professional interview. The thing is that as a single Christians we are constantly interviewing the opposite sex with our marriage-minded questions. When in our twenties the questions are more on the order of ...is he/she attractive, has interesting friends, fills in awkward pauses seamlessly, no body language red flags, educated, working etc.. In our thirties the interview questions become much more focused depending on the wisdom we gained in our twenties.

The church can help in generating some good discussion questions drawn from their pre-marital counseling courses for engaged couples. There are also some good questions to start out with in chapter 7: THEE LIST. For questions that generate good discussion (not marriage related) use the questions from this book located at the end of select sections. At the end of the date give each other feedback on his/her dating demeanor. Here are a few sample questions.

1 Do I talk about myself beyond what is enjoyable?
2 Do I divulge too much *sensitive* personal information out of context?
3 Do I talk about topics that are interesting?
4 Do I ask questions sincerely, not in a fact-finding or going down a list manner?
5 Do I maintain comfortable eye contact?
6 Do I interrupt you when you talk?
7 Do I listen to what you have to say?

8   Do I respect your opinions even though mine may differ?

9   Do I demonstrate impatience when you don't understand what I say?

10 Am I suitably engaged in my interests and/or hobbies?

11 Do I gossip?

12 Do I speak with appropriate volume and diction?

13 Is my dress appropriate and hygiene acceptable?

14 How are my table manners?

15 Do I have quirks that make me seem uncomfortable with myself?

16 Do I blink my eyes nervously when I talk?

This list in not intended to be all encompassing. So go ahead and add your own; your "date" with him may be your last opportunity to give him such things to think about for his betterment.

If you are convinced that you have found a "good egg," you might just request another "date" with him and give him a different set of evaluation questions to think about. What you are in essence communicating to each other is, "Here's a list of how to be sensitive to my peculiarities." After three or four such dates, if he is still interested in pursuing you, both of you will have made a "sensitivities list" for each other that will help guide your courtship behavior.

Afterword

So the take-home message of this book is to convince women that her role is to drop hints. You may still disagree with this role. Nevertheless, I feel obligated to paint a picture for you as a final motivational push to get you to believe me. I know this picture might be insensitive. But it is better for you to be prepared for your future so you are not too devastated if this scenario comes true for you.

Imagine yourself sitting in your oak rocking chair old, gray-haired and alone in your nursing home apartment. You are rocking forward and back; *creak, creak, creak, creak.* A smug grin on your face nestles among your deep facial wrinkles.

No family photos decorate your living room walls—no husband or married children and thus no grandchildren. In their place on the wall is a college degree, maybe even a master's or doctorate, plaques of accolades from your former employer of many, many years, and perhaps a few articles on you from a popular "who's who" magazine.

In addition, visible to no one else but you is your proud accomplishment of never having been dependent on anyone, especially not a man, for your success and security. You have never compromised your all-important "fiercely independent" image. You are destructively proud that you never lowered your personal standard of not looking "desperate" in front of any man. You are destructively proud that you never once let down your guard to expose your vulnerability. You are destructively proud that you never condescended to the time-tested tradition of dropping a godly, subtle hint to the man of your dreams. You may even ponder, "Whatever happened to that author who wrote that contentious book on dropping subtle hints?"

Yes, you are destructively proud that you were once very desirable and you probably think you still are, even in retirement. Yet you have only fleeting memories of being pursued and those memories are awkward at best. Indeed your own destructive pride has been preserved. *Creak, creak; creak, creak.*

Ouch! That hurts *me* reading it, and I already knew how it was going to end.

Now imagine a single man living out the above hypothetical scenario, one of the single men, David, that you crossed paths with in life. He also had a stellar professional career, raking in the awards and accolades just like the old woman (you) in the rocking chair. Sadly, he was a timid fellow, preferring to avoid awkward moments with women. He never asked out women on dates because he never felt their "permission" to do so. In his prime adult years it was politically correct in society to wait until a woman gave some kind of hint that she was interested. So he waited and waited. Meanwhile he employed his talents in his career, waiting and waiting. Now he sits an old man in his retirement home rocking chair alone, single. *Creak, creak; creak, creak.*

Continue imagining you are the old woman sitting in the rocking chair with all your degrees, accolades, etc. Now imagine in addition to the accolades hanging on your living room wall are pictures of your husband David, children, and grandchildren. We all would agree that you were an exceptionally blessed woman. She "had it all," says one of those "who's who" articles.

I don't know any man or woman who would say that you now an elderly woman wasted your time in life. The point is that *your* future can easily go from regretful old lonely woman to fulfilled and satisfied old woman by simply dropping your foolish destructive pride and instead dropping hints.

There are many good single Christian men around you just waiting for your hint. Many of them may even end up living down the hall from you in your retirement suite. But your memories of them will be as acquaintances at arm's length; never letting them closer than that.

Tomorrow, wherever you will be, I pray that you will try dropping a hint. It doesn't have to be perfectly polished; just try something *extremely* subtle to start out. But for the sake of your future love story, try *something*. Won't retirement life be so much nicer if you have a husband "David", children and grandchildren with whom to share it? Your "David" is waiting for your hint.